Managing the Internet Controversy

EDITED BY

Mark Smith

NEAL-SCHUMAN NETGUIDE SERIES

Neal-Schuman Publishers, Inc.

NEW YORK   *LONDON*

Published by Neal-Schuman Publishers, Inc.
100 Varick Street
New York, NY 10013

Printed and bound in the United States of America.

ISBN 1–55570–395–X

The paper used in this publication meets the minimum requirements of American National Standard for Information Sciences — Permanence of Paper for Printed Library Materials, ANSI Z39.48-1992.

Library of Congress Cataloging-in-Publication Data

Managing the internet controversy / edited by Mark L. Smith
    p. cm.
Includes bibliographical references and index.
    ISBN 1-55570-395-X (alk. paper) — (Neal-Schuman
NetGuide Series)
       1. Internet access for library users—United States. 2. Internet—
Access control—United States. 3. Information technology—
Social aspects—United States. 4. Information society.
I. Smith, Mark, 1956– II. Series

Z692.C65 M365 2001
025.04—dc21   00-062516

Table of Contents

Preface

More has been said about the Internet in libraries—in the library press, in newspapers, on talk radio, and in the tabloids—than any other phenomenon ever associated with libraries. Librarians, patrons, public officials, parents, and every member of the concerned public know that offering access to the Internet changes libraries. Often they do not know this change has been mainly for the good. Yet in spite of all the ink, bandwidth, and hot air this topic has generated, there has been surprisingly little written for library staff and advocates on how to cope with Internet access in libraries. *Managing the Internet Controversy* is written by the best and brightest of the library profession: people who have coped with the controversy both in the trenches of public service as well as the most prominent levels of the public dialogue.

The public is making every imaginable use of the Internet in the library. Every day they use interactive games, pop e-mail, chat sessions, and MP3 downloads. They view every imaginable type of material, from the lofty sort of research envisioned by the inventors of the medium over 30 years ago to the basest sort of prurient content offensive to the majority of citizens, including many library staff. Offensive yes, but illegal? In all but a handful of very specific cases, the answer is no. We need to remember that the law of the land is the United States Constitution, which prohibits government restrictions on the content of what adults can see, read, and discuss. This point is sometimes difficult to convey to parents, elected and appointed officials, and other influential community or campus leaders. Harder still to digest is the notion, upheld by the courts, that even children have specific constitutional rights to read and view a broad range of materials regardless of what opinion their parents may have of that material.

Last year, radio talk show host Laura Schlessinger (Dr. Laura to her listeners) began attacking the American Library Association for its stated positions on anti-filtering and the assertion that adults should have free access to materials in the library regardless of medium. She incited parents and other concerned listeners to demand of local libraries that they protect children from "pornography" in the library. If libraries chose not to respond affirmatively to the demands for filtered Internet access, she recommended that her listeners actively oppose funding for those libraries. Her tactic worked most visibly in the state of Colorado in 1999 when Governor Bill Owens vetoed a bill that would have provided an additional two million dollars in statewide funding for libraries—a decision delivered at the height of the controversy generated by Dr. Laura. Other visible manifestations of the Internet controversy have been played out locally in such communities as Holland, Michigan (a public referendum on filtering in the public library); Loudoun County, Virginia (a landmark court case); Livermore, California (details to come); and Medina, Ohio (where a public library director resigned over the controversy); and in dozens of other communities across the nation, perhaps your own.

The Internet controversy has been useful to this extent: it has forced a new level of introspection within the profession. The ruckus over Internet content forced acute examination of several important issues. How do librarians maintain core professional values that may seem out of step with common sense demands of their communities? Is there a compromise that protects both children's safety and intellectual freedom? What words can the librarian say to the media, the mayor, the library board, the parent, or the public about library Internet access that will calm the waters rather than pour fuel on the flame?

Practical questions effect library staff and services every day. How can librarians plan for the controversy and manage the consequences? What do you say when the phone rings? How do you respond to the allegation that you are a pornographer because you do not filter? How do you craft a strategy that allows your staff to speak sensibly to the public, casts the library as a responsible community partner, and plans for the systematic growth of Internet use as a library resource?

Developing clear policies is one successful early indication. A recently released study by the Library Research Service and the Library School of the University of Illinois indicates that 94 percent of libraries offering Internet access also have Internet policies. But policies prove helpful only so far as we have anticipated all scenarios. Policies can never be absolute and even the best rely on procedures, staff involvement, and the ongoing interaction with a public that can sometimes be quirky, demanding, and unpredictable.

Managing the Internet Controversy is a collection of essays by prominent librarians in the profession today. Represented are four presidents of the American Library Association, two presidents of the Freedom to Read Foundation, a *Library Journal* Librarian of the Year, a president of the American Association of School Librarians, and other spirited library leaders. Each of these authors has struggled first hand—either on the local, state, or national level (sometimes all three!)—with the challenges and opportunities as they integrated use of the Internet into the life of the library .

The dozen chapters of *Managing the Internet Controversy* begin with a survey by Nancy Kranich, academic librarian, ALA President, and author of dozens of articles on the topic of digital libraries, of the status of Internet access and use in this country, current laws governing use, and the role libraries can play in addressing what has come to be known as the "digital divide." Another ALA President and public librarian, Sarah Long, and co-author Melissa Henderson, tackle the similar but distinct topic of how the library's use of the Internet builds communities. Judith Krug, longtime director of the ALA office of Intellectual Freedom who has led the profession in defining its values regarding First Amendment issues, describes how those values continue to prevail in the era of electronic access.

Three authors provide highly practical advice for using the Internet with children. Former ALA President and school librarian Ann Symons provides sensible recommendations on ways to work with parents to head off controversy before it begins. Carolyn Noah describes techniques for helping children learn to use the Internet as a legitimate information resource. M. Ellen Jay provides a step-by-step case study in the introduction of Internet service in her school library.

Three articles on speaking to others about the Internet are offered. Gordon Conable, a respected public library administrator and former President of the Freedom to Read Foundation, describes how to work with trustees to build a level of cooperation and trust that will withstand controversy. Patricia Glass Schuman, former ALA President, author, and library literature publisher, offers pointers on how to become media savvy when talking to the press about library Internet access. I tackle the topic of how to work with elected officials—especially state legislators—to effectively argue for funding to expand online services while managing controversial questions that often arise in these interactions.

Carolyn Caywood, well known to many readers for her column in *School Library Journal*, explores how to prepare staff for all aspects of Internet service including training, supervision, and answering tough questions from the public. In her essay on "Ethics and the Internet," Susan Fuller, a *Library Journal* Librarian of the Year, provides a case history in the novel approach of using professional mediation to negotiate a solution to the controversy of Internet access and filtering in her library. The volume closes with a final case study in public library Internet access in the Fort Vancouver, Washington, Public Library by Candace Morgan, a President of the Freedom to Read Foundation.

These cutting-edge ideas will certainly contribute a good read on the topic of Internet in libraries, furnishing thought-provoking ideas as well as practical advice.

Managing the Internet Controversy aims to support any librarian facing the controversies that inevitably arise when organizations take great risks for great rewards

RESOURCES

LaRue, James. 1999 "Colorado's Governor Doesn't Get It." *Library Journal* 124 (July 1999): p64.

Library Research Center and the Graduate School of Library and Information Science, University of Illinois. 2000. *Survey of Internet Access Management in Public Libraries*. Denver: Library Research Service.

Chapter 1

Libraries, the Internet, and Democracy

Nancy Kranich

LIBRARIES AND DEMOCRACY

Democracies need libraries. Since their inception, libraries have served as pivotal community institutions upholding, strengthening, and realizing some of the most fundamental democratic ideals of our society. Libraries are the only American institutions that make knowledge, ideas, and information freely available to all citizens. They are the place where people can find differing opinions on controversial questions and dissent from current orthodoxy. They serve as the source for the pursuit of independent thought, critical attitudes, and in-depth information. And in so doing, they guard against the tyranny of ignorance, the Achilles' heel of every democracy.

An informed public constitutes the very foundation of a democracy; after all, democracies are about discourse, discourse among the people. Consequently, the pursuit of knowledge and self-enlightenment lies at the heart of this democracy. That is, if a free society is to survive, it must ensure the preservation and provision of accessible knowledge for all its citizens. Note that libraries in a free society perform the fundamental function of keeping the public well informed. Libraries are the cornerstone of democracy in our communities because they assist the public in locating a diversity of resources and in developing the information literacy skills necessary to become responsible, informed citizens and to participate in our democracy. As James Madison eloquently stated: "A popular Government, without popular information, or the means of acquiring it, is but a prologue to a farce or a tragedy; or, perhaps, both. Knowledge will forever govern ignorance and a people who mean to be their own governors must arm themselves with the power knowledge gives."

Libraries ensure the freedom of speech, the freedom to read, the freedom to view. A true democratic institution, libraries are for everyone, everywhere—no one should be excluded. They provide safe spaces for public dialogue. They provide the resources needed for the public to inform itself, in order to participate in every aspect of our information society. They disseminate information so the public can participate in self governance. They provide access to government information so that the public can monitor the work of its elected officials and benefit from the data collected and disseminated by public policy makers.

In America, libraries were "invented" and exist in order to give all people equal access to learning and self-determination. Libraries are uniquely democratic.

LIBRARIES AND CIVIL SOCIETY

As libraries serve to prepare citizens for a lifetime of civic participation, they also encourage the development of civil society. They provide the information and the opportunities for dialogue that the public needs to make decisions about common concerns. As community forums, they encourage active citizenship and renew communities. When people are better informed, they are more likely to participate in policy discussions where they can communicate their ideas and concerns freely. Most important, citizens need civic spaces where they can speak freely, share similar interests and concerns, and pursue what they believe is in their interest.

Effective citizen action is possible when citizens develop the skills to gain access to information of all kinds and to put such information to effective use. Librarians teach the public how to identify and evaluate information that is essential to making decisions that affect the way they live, work, learn, and govern themselves. Beyond the individual, libraries also provide the real and virtual spaces for members of the community to exchange ideas—ideas fundamental to democratic participation and civil society. Ultimately, discourse among informed citizens assures civil society; and civil society provides the social capital necessary to achieve sovereignty of the people, by the people, and for the people. In recent years, the essential processes of democracy have undergone serious rethinking, led by Robert Putnam's analysis of social capital and its relationship to civic participation cum civil society. See, for example, "Bowling Alone: America's Declining Social Capital."

THE INFORMATION RICH AND THE INFORMATION POOR

No city in the world enjoys such rich cultural and information resources as my home town—New York. And no city contains so many rich residents. At the same time, New York also harbors some of the poorest people in America, impoverished not just by their incomes, but also by their lack of access to the wealth of information and other cultural resources that surround them. While the digital age promises the potential of closing this gap between rich and poor, the haves and have-nots will likely grow further apart in the race to dominate commerce in the digital age. Electronic entrepreneurs become millionaires overnight and science and knowledge advances at break-neck speed. Nevertheless, this new age of abundance, now stripping away the ravages of scarcity, has yet to benefit many of those left behind and to close the gap between the information rich and information poor.

While e-commerce creates a new class of information rich, many of New York's children suffer poor reading abilities. School libraries lack both books and professional staff to improve reading scores, even though studies have proven that good school media programs increase learning. Twenty percent of American adults do not read well enough to earn a living wage. Public libraries in New York lose one-quarter of their staff each year because of low salaries and, thus, barely supplement the poor services offered to children in the schools.

By contrast, New York boasts a magnificent new Science and Industry Library with access to electronic databases that many of the Fortune 500 companies lack, and a refurbished Humanities Center that is the envy of all America. The public libraries have worked hard to supplement their diverse collections and services by providing Internet and electronic database access in branches located in virtually every neighborhood in the city. But demand for unfettered access dramatically outstrips supply; and, regrettably, too much of this demand results from New York's poor-quality school libraries which are forced to filter the Internet, severely limiting access to the most basic resources.

Indeed, college students at private universities in the city wallow in lush, extensive library collections supplemented by thousands of licensed electronic tools, while students at public universities have barely the books or electronic databases to complete their class assignments, let alone advance scholarship. As a compensation, libraries should offer the equal opportunities Americans seek to succeed in the information society; yet libraries are stressed to the limit in their abilities to deliver on this covenant.

This is a hard story to tell, but there is reason for optimism. The Internet promises to bridge the gap between the information haves and have-nots in New York and elsewhere. No longer divided by geographic, linguistic, or economic barriers, electronic information can span boundaries, and reach into any neighborhood with just the click of a mouse. Truly, the dream of an equitable information society offers new hope for rekindling the democratic principles put forth by our founding fathers in the Constitution. Even if a household cannot afford nor chooses not to connect to the Internet, families have the option of logging on at a library or school. Under the universal service provisions of the Telecommunications Act of 1996, nearly every community will soon be connected, thus ensuring an on-ramp to the information superhighway, providing an opportunity for everyone to participate in their communities' economic, educational, social, political, and leisure activities.

The Clinton Administration has drawn the nation's attention to the "Digital Divide" and the gap between the information rich and poor in America. Recent research indicates that, despite a significant increase in computer ownership and overall usage, many low income, minority, disabled, rural, and inner city groups are falling behind in their ownership of computers and access to telecommunications networks. And, beyond the purchase of hardware and connectivity to the Internet, librarians have stepped into this gap to ensure public access to a broad array of information resources, promoting literacy in the twenty-first century, and reducing barriers to intellectual freedom and fair use.

THE DIGITAL CONTENT DIVIDE

Into the milieu of this new century comes the Internet with affordable and accessible content, content that was previously unavailable to many communities, both in the United States and abroad. However, access to an abundance of information does not necessarily mean access to a diversity of sources. Cyberspace is sparse when it comes to local information, particularly for rural communities and those living at or near the poverty level. The vast majority of Internet sites are designed for people with average or advanced literacy levels. For the more than 20 percent of Americans whose reading levels limit them to poverty wages and for the 30 million Americans speaking a language other than English, few Websites are readily comprehended. Furthermore, ethnic and racial minorities are unlikely to find content about the uniqueness of their cultures. A recent report by The Children's Partnership estimated that at least 50 million Americans—roughly 20 percent—faced a content-related barrier that stood between them and the benefits of the Internet. For example, in March 2000 only three Websites could be found for institutions operating in Harlem. The Children's Partnership study also indicates that adults wanted practical information focusing on local community, information at a basic literacy level, content for non-English speakers, and racial and ethnic cultural information. It also found that Internet use among low-income Americans was for self-improvement, whether for online courses, job search, or other information. In short, the poor and marginalized individuals seek information that helps them with their day-to-day problems and enables them to participate as members of their democratic community (The Children's Partnership, 2000).

Libraries are well positioned to meet these needs. Targeting Websites and digital library development toward special populations is crucial if we are to ensure widespread participation in the information society. We must ensure that sites are easy to navigate, translated into languages spoken by residents, and responsive to local needs. Information equity must become a priority for the entire community. We must purchase licensed materials and convert older items that contain content of interest to those at the margins of our communities. Libraries must join forces with community groups and institutions to bridge the digital content divide.

INFORMATION LITERACY IN A HIGHLY MEDIATED WORLD

Copyright registrations now exceed 560,000 per year. New book titles published annually in the United States have jumped more than 30 percent over the last decade. More than 100,000 federal and 10,000 United Nations documents enter circulation annually, along with untold numbers of state and local documents.

Even more astounding is the exponential growth of the World Wide Web. A February 1999 study reported in *Nature* concluded there were about 800 million publicly available Web pages, with about 15 trillion bytes of textual information and 180 million images weighing in at about three trillion bytes of data. The rapid growth of the Web is estimated to be slightly more than double in size every year, though some sources estimate that it doubles every six months (Lawrence and Giles, 1998). As of this writing in April, 2000, the Censorware home page reported that the Internet included: 1,820,000,000 Web pages and 409,000,000 images; and that the lifespan of a Web page is about 44 days, which means that 41,300,000 pages and

9,300,000 images change daily. In just the last 24 hours, the Web has added 3,690,000 new pages and 831,000 new images. The Censorware Project home page provides a daily count on Web size at *www.censorware.org/web_size/*.

Yet as many librarians know too well, much of the information available over the Internet is either erroneous or tailors its information to advocate a position; there is no validation like peer review to guide users. Much of the "good" information is licensed and restricted to those who have invested and contracted for access. Not surprisingly, the complexity of finding, evaluating, and utilizing information in the electronic age has become a major challenge for the 60 percent of the workforce which engages in some information-related activity. Librarians are needed more than ever to ensure that the public has the information literacy skills it needs to live, work, learn, and govern in the digital age.

Americans need sophisticated information literacy skills to succeed in the twenty-first century. Even those already proficient at finding, evaluating, and applying information to solve daily problems can be overwhelmed by the proliferation of information and the difficulty of sorting through it. To cope successfully, citizens must be able to identify, evaluate, apply information, and communicate it efficiently and effectively. Americans will have to become information literate to flourish in the workplace as well as to carry out the day-to-day activities of citizens in a developed, democratic society. Libraries of all types must work together to develop a process to engage community groups in identifying information needs, to initiate a dialogue aimed at encouraging a more information literate populace, and to facilitate the development of skills to utilize information strategically. Granted, the need for information literacy skills has been around for generations; nevertheless, the dawning of the information society forces us to develop broader information skills if we are to separate the wheat from the chaff, the true from the untrue, the rumor from the real.

In the contemporary environment of rapid technological change and proliferating information resources, communities face diverse, abundant information choices. The uncertain quality and expanding quantity of information pose large challenges for society. The sheer abundance of information will not in itself create a more informed citizenry without a complementary cluster of abilities necessary to use information effectively.

COMMUNITY NETWORKS

Comparable to libraries, community networks—such as freenets—create channels of communication for public dialogue. The movement toward community networks reflects the desire for a democratic institution capable of recognizing the centrality of information access and communication to modern life. Here too, libraries have led. Working closely with a broad array of community partners, the conceptualization of these networks derives directly from the model of the public library. Community networks offer many of the services provided by libraries, including training, e-mail, Web page development, and small business assistance. They also focus users on local assets and services, pulling together essential information and communication resources that might otherwise be difficult to identify or locate. Of special interest here, they offer opportunities for libraries to collaborate and build partnerships in support of local history projects, civic education programs, and community enterprises—such as information and referral services—that might be overlooked by the commercial sector. Significantly, librarians bring added value to this movement by offering skills and expertise to those who sustain these ventures. Especially for public libraries, community networks offer an exceptional opportunity to forge new roles in their communities.

GOVERNMENT INFORMATION

Over the last decade, the persistent voice of librarians and the promise of new technologies have improved access to government information. The result has been the promotion of the public's right to know along with the advancement of citizens' involvement in governance. A 15–year struggle to promote equal, ready, and equitable access to government information culminated in passage of the GPO Access Act, the Electronic Freedom of Information Act, and other policies endeavoring to strengthen public access in the digital age. Still, the victory has been incomplete. While the public benefits from ever more direct access to government records and documents (witness the speed with which the unedited version of Kenneth Starr's report reached citizens' hands) more and more data was slipping into private hands, getting classified under the guise of national security, or exempted from release under the Freedom of Information Act. Just last year, a proposal to ensure permanent public access to electronic government documents was forwarded by the library community to Congress and promptly ignored. At that very moment, links to important documents disappeared unnoticed, and a court of appeals allowed federal agencies to destroy electronic documents resident in word processing or e-mail systems once a copy is made for record keeping. So while public access to government information produced at taxpayer expense is more freely available than ever before, the threat to public access persists. Yet even more vulnerable, state and local electronic information rarely falls under depository and other open access statutes. We should savor our victories while recognizing that we must remain vigilant and continue the struggle for truly open access.

COPYRIGHT AND FAIR USE

Against the promise of easy access to networked electronic information loom new technological protection measures. The ubiquity of digital information, the widespread use of networks, and the proliferation of the World Wide Web create new tensions in the intellectual property arena. The ease with which data may be copied impels information producers to seek ways of protecting their investments. Their intentions are perfectly understandable. Unfortunately, measures proposed to protect creators endanger users' fair-use rights to view, reproduce, and quote limited amounts of copyrighted materials. This high-stakes policy debate might well result in a pay-per-view, or—even more chilling—a pay-per-slice digital information economy where only those willing and able to pay can access electronic information. With librarians in the vanguard, the delicate balance between creators' and users' rights to information has been carefully negotiated for print materials over the past century. However, as we enter the Information Age, the balance has begun to tilt toward intellectual property owners. Should this imbalance persist, it will endanger free speech, the promotion of learning, and the rekindling of civil society.

The Digital Millennium Copyright Act of 1998 criminalizes illegal use of digital materials for the first time and places additional limits on the rights of electronic information users. As a consequence, the widespread deployment of pay-per-view systems could effectively reduce libraries from repositories of valuable knowledge to mere marketing platforms for content distributors. Fair use was only negotiated into the bill after librarians and public interest activists threatened to defeat it. Subsequently, fair use barely survived as new restrictions were imposed on unauthorized access to technologically restricted work. The act prohibits the "circumvention" of any effective "technological protection measure" (TPMs) used by a copyright holder to restrict access to its material unless adverse affects on the fair use of any class of work can be demonstrated. Thus, the burden of proof rests with those of us seeking open access and the free flow of information.

A second copyright-related bill, the Collections of Information Antipiracy Act, will protect investment rather than creativity for database companies and overturn over 200 years of information policy that has consistently supported unfettered access to factual information. This bill draws its support from a small but powerful group of database publishers including Lexis-Nexis (owned by Reed-Elsevier), the New York Stock Exchange, and the National Association of Realtors, and will allow a producer or publisher unprecedented control over the uses of information, including factual information as well as government works. Even though the Supreme Court has held that constitutional copyright principles prohibit ownership of facts or works of the federal government and current copyright law already protects database companies, some corporations continue to press hard for this over-broad protectionist legislation. Should they succeed, they will accomplish a radical departure from the current intellectual property framework that protects expression—not investment—and thereby endanger the doctrine of fair use. If these special interests prevail, we will wind up with a pay-per-view digital economy where the free flow of ideas is limited to the obsolescent world of print and photocopy machines.

UNIVERSAL SERVICE AND FILTERING

Since the early decades of the twentieth century, Americans have held the belief that maximum access to public information sources and channels of communication is necessary for political, economic, and social participation in a vigorous democracy. Everyone must have access to information communication networks in order to participate in our democratic way of life. Under the universal service provisions of the Telecommunications Act of 1996, the Federal Communications Commission has authorized a program to ensure equitable access to telecommunications technologies by offering schools and libraries discounted rates that were once reserved for only the largest corporate customers. In this way, schools and libraries may be connected as a first step toward widespread public access. Known as the E-rate, over two billion dollars in discounts and grants is now earmarked annually for distribution from fees collected by long distance phone carriers. In addition, the E-rate helps bridge the digital divide by expanding access and connectivity to needy communities (*www.ala.org/washoff/e-rate.html*). Still, it took some horse-trading to gain acceptance for the E-rate. Telecommunications companies agreed to this amendment to the 1996 Telecommunications Act in return for deregulation of their markets. Even so, several of the major carriers who benefited most from deregulation have tried to sabotage this program through court challenges and by highlighting the universal service charge on consumer bills without explanation, thereby inciting their enormous customer base.

Where corporate attempts to stop the flow of subsidies to schools and libraries ends, Congress has added its own twists. A number of bills that require local communities to install filters to protect children from obscenity and child pornography as a condition of receiving E-rate subsidies threaten the feasibility of the funds. Attempts to tie federal funding to content restrictions raise serious constitutional questions similar to those brought forward in the *ACLU v Reno* case which challenged the constitutionality of the Communications Decency Act. These bills will impose federal regulations over local community control of information access. First Amendment protections must extend to the digital sphere if we are to ensure open dialogue across the full spectrum of opinion in the Information Age.

Many states have proposed similar laws to restrict Internet access in schools and libraries by mandating a filtering requirement in order for these institutions to receive state and local funding. Unfortunately, filters do more harm than good; they sweep too broadly, blocking only some of the sites with indecent materials while restricting access to legal and useful resources. In those few libraries that currently employ filters, users complain that they block such home pages as the Super Bowl XXX, the Mars Exploration site (MARSEXPL), a site on swan migration in Alma, Wis. (swANALma), *Mother Jones* magazine, the National Rifle Association, and millions of other sites of legitimate interest. Filtering systems have trouble distinguishing between users who are 6 and 16 years old, which applies the common denominator of the youngest users at the expense of all others. Furthermore, filters are not effective in blocking much material that some consider undesirable for children; they give parents a false sense of security leading them to believe that their children are protected from harm; and, most importantly, they do not take the place of preferred routes that include the development of community-based Internet Access Policies, user education programs, links to great sites, and safety guidelines. The extraordinary benefits of Internet access are too often overshadowed by controversies fueled by groups who stoke imagined fears about the power of images and words in an effort to control access to information. According to a recent study by the National Coalition Against Censorship, "the evidence of harm from Internet access at public institutions is at best equivocal, and the blunt-edged approach advocated by pro-censorship advocates ignores the individualized need of children and their parents. Fortunately, most libraries have found ways of balancing the interests of all parties effectively, without censorship . . ." (National Coalition Against Censorship, 1999).

THE TIDE OF THE INFORMATION AGE

Over the last 20 years, with the emergence of personal computers and telecommunications technologies, we have seen a transformation of the information creation, transport, and dissemination industries from independent operators mostly involved with infrastructure to a highly integrated, multinational sphere of megacompanies looking to optimize profits and dominate access to home and business. In the U.S., a period of deregulation and privatization has shifted the information policymaking arena to the private sector where questions of the public interest are harder to raise.

What is at stake is not only the availability and affordability of information essential to the public interest, but also the very basis upon which local libraries serve the public's information needs. As communications and media industry giants stake their claims in cyberspace, the public interest must not be overlooked. The new information infrastructure must ensure public spaces that are filled by educational and research institutions, libraries, non-profits, and governmental organizations charged with promoting and fulfilling public policy goals. They must constitute a public sphere of free speech and open intellectual discourse which enhances democracy.

If the public's right to know is to be protected within a free-market national information infrastructure, the library community must work together with public groups, who must stand up and speak out for the public interest. Librarians are well positioned to lead the charge because we are committed to ensuring the free flow of information in our society and we understand what is at stake. Librarians have already staked a claim in the newly emerging national information infrastructure. After all, we are the information professionals who represent more than half of the country's adults as well as three-quarters of its children who use libraries. Librarians excel at identifying, acquiring, organizing, housing, preserving, archiving, and assisting in the use of information. We have extensive experience working with community groups in providing essential local information and promoting the public's right to know. Furthermore, local libraries serve as the community's historic, cultural, political, and social record and are identified as a center for reflection and stimulation by area residents. We inform citizens about the activities of their local, state, and federal governments through depository and other government information dissemination programs.

What the library community brings to the information infrastructure issue is the perspective of cooperative, not competitive, information professionals serving the public interest. Politically neutral institutions, libraries are charged with strengthening democracy by facilitating public access to information in all its forms. The library mission includes providing such access regardless of a person's economic status, education level, or information-seeking skills. In an electronic age, this mission requires equal, ready, and equitable access to the nation's telecommunications infrastructure, access that will be even more crucial in the future. Without technologically sophisticated libraries available in every community, the evolving information infrastructure can only intensify the gulf between the information rich and the information poor.

LIBRARIANS LEADING THE CHARGE FOR PUBLIC ACCESS

Librarians must act quickly and decisively to affect the ever-growing policy issues that will change the means by which information is produced and distributed. Neutrality will not work; the stakes are very high—namely, our democratic way of life that depends upon an informed electorate. We must recognize why these issues are so important. We must be informed about the issues and the players on all sides; and we cannot be effective on our own. We must work together with others to make a difference. We must enter the struggle adequately armed. We must make every effort to balance the influence of a well-organized corporate community. We must build coalitions to promote public access, to increase our strength and influence, and to galvanize grassroots action.

The promises of the 21st-century information society must not be placed in peril by those content on restricting public access to information and the free flow of ideas. A high-tech society must not become a highly controlled society. The vigilance and activism of those concerned with protecting free expression is more important than ever if the American ideals embedded in the First Amendment of the Constitution are to remain the beacon of our way of life in the new millennium. We must speak up and fight for information equity for all. Otherwise, we will endanger our most precious right in a democratic society—the right of free speech and inquiry.

RESOURCES

"Accessibility of Information on the Web," *Nature* 400 (July 8, 1999): 107–109.

American Library Association, Office of Intellectual Freedom Website. Available: *www.ala.org/oif.html*.

American Library Association Washington Office Website, *www.ala.org/washoff/copyright.html*, provides up-to-date information about copyright issues and links to numerous other sites concerned with protecting fair use in the digital age.

The Benton Foundation. 1998. *What's Going On, Losing Ground Bit by Bit: Low-Income Communities in the Information Age*. [Online]. Available: *www.benton.org/Library/Low-Income/*.

The Children's Partnership. 2000. *Online Content for Low-Income and Underserved Americans: The Digital Divide's New Frontier–A Strategic Audit of Activities and Opportunities* [Online]. Available: *www.childrens partnership.org/*.

Durrance, Joan, and Karen Pettigrew. 2000. "Community Information: The Technological Touch," *Library Journal*: 44–46.

The Freedom to Read Foundation Website, *www.ftrf.org/index.html*.

Lawrence, S., and C. L. Giles. 1998. "Searching the World Wide Web," *Science* 280: 98.

The National Coalition Against Censorship. 1999. *The Cyber-Library: Legal and Policy Issues Facing Public Libraries in the High-Tech Era*. New York: NCAC: 8. Available: *www.ncac.org/cyberlibrary.html*.

Novak, Thomas P., and Donna L. Hoffman. 1998. "Bridging the Digital Divide: The Impact of Race on Computer Access and Internet Use," Vanderbilt University e-lab manuscripts (February 2) [Online]. Available: *www 2000.ogsm.vanderbilt.edu/papers/race/science.html*.

Putnam, Robert. 1995. "Bowling Alone: America's Declining Social Capital." *Journal of Democracy* 6: 65–78.

Schuler, Douglas. 1996. *New Community Networks: Wired for Change,* Reading, MA: Addison-Wesley.

Schuler, Douglas. 1997. "Let's Partner as Patriots: The Future of Democracy May Lie in Linking Libraries with Community Networks." *American Libraries* (September): 60–62.

U.S. Department of Commerce, National Telecommunications and Information Administration. 1995, 1998, 1999. *Falling Through the Net: Defining the Digital Divide.* Available: *www.ntia.doc.gov/ntiahom/fttn99/*.

Chapter 2

How Libraries Use the Internet to Build Communities

Sarah Ann Long and Melissa Henderson

As the online world grows and expands, it has become as easy—if not easier—to contact a friend or relative on the other side of the globe as it is to chat with our next-door neighbor. As access to global information grows and expands, worries have arisen that citizens are, in fact, losing touch with their next-door neighbor, the local shopkeepers, and the local librarian. Reports and articles, such as Robert Putnam's much-publicized "Bowling Alone," highlight the decrease in interaction between community members. Many scholars and pundits point to the Internet as one of the key culprits; painting a picture of the lone citizen sitting in front of the glowing screen, surfing the world without ever looking out of the window or walking down the street.

The brighter side of this picture depicts the community-building aspects of the Internet. Technologies such as e-mail, bulletin boards, and chat groups bring diverse groups of people together. Websites provide information when people want it; opening and closing hours no longer present service limitations to customers. Technology can help overcome physical obstacles presented by geography, transportation, or even disability.

More than just providing information, the Internet is helping build communities, both physical and virtual. The Internet offers us a number of ways to connect with others, from such simple technologies as e-mail to more advanced applications such as online chat. Many early online communities were developed using bulletin board technologies. Users would dial into a specific computer and read and post messages on a given topic. Many people are familiar with The Well (Whole Earth 'Lectronic Link), a pioneering online community started 1985, and the ubiquitous and diverse Usenet Newsgroups. These resources developed communities of avocation and vocation that brought together far-flung people who shared similar interests. Bulletin boards also appealed to members of various groups who may not have been able to communicate freely in public, allowing the opportunity to interact, talk, and commiserate from the comfort and anonymity of their own home.

E-mail has also been widely used as both a broadcast (one to many) and an interactive (many to many) community building tool. Organizations and individuals send out newsletters on subjects of interest. Individuals subscribe to e-mail discussion groups covering a range of topics. Suddenly, someone with a relatively obscure interest can communicate with hundreds of other like-minded individuals around the world.

Commercial services such as CompuServe and America Online quickly realized the value of these online communities and made them a central part of their offerings. Online bulletin boards were set up for a range of topics and interests, both professional and personal. Commercial online services engaged staff to serve as hosts of various topic areas. Hosts would encourage new members to participate, offer instruction on both the written and unwritten rules of the community, and discourage behavior defined as inappropriate by that community. Before long, corporations and businesses began recognizing the value of the community-building aspects of the online world. Companies quickly realized that they couldn't simply post Web pages and expect consumers to make return visits to their Websites, let alone regularly purchase their products online. Web visitors needed to interact with the organization or, better yet, with other consumers interested in that product or service.

Many of the early online community-building efforts were purely entertaining, such as the Ragu spaghetti sauce site which offered an online game in which visitors tried to help "Mama" feed as many family members as possible. Community-building resources have grown more content-oriented in recent years. Some well-known examples include reader reviews at the online bookseller Amazon.com and the ratings service at online auction site ebay.com. In both of these cases, the vendor isn't the expert; members of the (buying) community are the voices of experience.

LIBRARIES AND COMMUNITY

The library building has long been the center of the community—the place where children and adults go to find information as well as intellectual, entertainment, and social activities. When looking for the *Encyclopedia Britannica* or the latest Stephen King short story, citizens are used to going into the library and browsing through the stacks. The development of the Internet, specifically the World Wide Web, has dramatically changed this method of information access. Both the *Encyclopedia Britannica* and the latest Stephen King novel are now available on the Web.

Is the role of the library changing? Can it remain the center of the community—physical and virtual—as these new technologies evolve? Many libraries are answering affirmatively and are employing online community-building tools to maintain their role. The remainder of this chapter will offer examples of tools and technologies that are currently being employed by libraries to build community. Each of these tools gives libraries the opportunity to serve their patrons in a new way—24 hours a day, 7 days a week. Additionally, many of these tools offer patrons the opportunity to directly interact with library resources without mediation, either individually or with other members of the community.

LIBRARIES AND E-MAIL

E-mail is a natural tool for libraries to adopt. Just as reference librarians adapted to receiving questions via telephone, they are now working out methods for fielding queries via e-mail. Like many libraries, the Daniel Boone Regional Library in Columbia, Missouri, offers an ask-a-librarian feature *(dbrl.library.missouri.org/reference/ref-question.html)* on their Website. Patrons are invited to submit queries using a simple online form. Of course, the global nature of the Internet places a new wrinkle in the policy-making process. Many libraries clearly state that e-mail reference questions from members of their communities will be handled with priority over queries from those outside of the library's service area. And, the immediate and round-the-clock nature of the Internet means that libraries need to clearly state how quickly e-mail queries can be answered. The Greenwich (Connecticut) Public Library offers a good example of e-mail reference policies on their Website at *www.greenwich.lib.ct.us/info/askusa.htm*. They address a variety of issues, including response time, confidentiality, and acceptable types of queries.

The Blue Island (Illinois) Public Library is using e-mail as a broadcast medium. Their Website *(www.blueisland. org/bipl/ebookworm.html)* encourages visitors to have "library happenings delivered directly to your e-mail box" via the Electric Bookworm, an e-mail–based newsletter. The Fort Smith (Arkansas) Public Library also offers a series of e-newsletters covering current events, building updates, computer training, and new library materials. These services allow patrons to stay informed of library goings-on and gives the library the opportunity to build an e-mail–based mailing list for other purposes such as surveys (with permission, of course). Another not-so-obvious benefit of this type of service is that it allows part-time citizens (such as retirees or summer residents) or former residents to stay in touch with their local library and the community. Offering an e-mail newsletter also can be a service to the profession; librarians across the country can subscribe to each other's newsletters and pick up ideas for programs or services to offer.

The La Grange (Illinois) Public Library has taken the unique step of offering e-postcards on their Website (*www.nsn.org/cgi-bin/lgs/postcard.pl*). This is an unmediated service in which the library's Web visitors communicate and interact with each other through the library Website, but without the intervention or participation of library staff. Steve Moskal, Director of the La Grange Public Library notes that the e-postcards "require no significant staff time and help to provide another connection between the user and library. It's a user-friendly service that is unexpected, but that has been well-received" (e-mail communication, March 29, 2000).

LIBRARIES AND GUESTBOOKS

Just as a blank wall encouraged "Kilroy" to leave a message, online guestbooks appeal to the graffiti artist in all of us. While not truly interactive, an online guestbook can give a Web visitor the sense of having communicated with the library responsible for the Website. The Santa Monica (California) Public Library offers a guestbook on their Website (*www.smpl.org/library/guestbook/addguest.shtml*). Entries in this library's guestbook illustrate the value of the Website and the library to current community members as well as to former citizens of Santa Monica.

Barrington Area (Illinois) Public Library has taken guestbook technology one step further. This library allows

Web visitors to offer book or video reviews in the "Reader Reviews" section of the Website (*www.bal.alibrary.com/ Adult_Services/reviews.htm*). There is no need for intervention or mediation by library staff; rather, this Web resource helps the library step into the role of bringing community members together to share insights and ideas under the umbrella of a comfortable and familiar organization.

LIBRARIES AND OTHER ONLINE COMMUNITY TOOLS

Like other organizations, libraries are becoming aware of the increasing requests for on-demand information in electronic format. Providing information and resources in a variety of formats 24 hours a day can help libraries retain their central role in the community. If neither time nor geography restricts patron's access to information, they can continue to turn to the library for their information needs.

Newsletters

One of the easiest things a library can do is offer an online edition of its newsletter. Many libraries, such as the Crystal Lake Area (Illinois) Public Library, archive their newsletters online.

Online catalogs

Many libraries offer their catalogs online, allowing patrons to search for resources; some even give patrons the ability to place holds on materials currently checked out or on

order. The Jefferson County (Alabama) Library Cooperative allows patrons to renew materials online, while other
libraries are beginning to discuss patron-initiated interli-
brary loan opportunities. Mount Prospect (Illinois) Public
Library allows patrons to register for library programs
online. These services demonstrate how libraries can continue to respond to their community's needs and play a
key information role without the direct mediation of a library staff member. According to Marilyn Genther, Executive Director of the Mount Prospect Public Library, "the
provision of an online service is in response to our changing society where so much is happening online and being
demanded on the spot. Twenty-four hours a day and seven
days a week access is expected. If libraries don't . . . have
a variety of options to access services, they will lose out."

Public information kiosks

Libraries can also help citizens log on to the Internet from
some rather unusual locations, such as the local shopping
mall or the grocery store. Public information kiosks link
people to community information networks, maps, government information, and library catalogs. The Baltimore
City (Maryland) Public Library offers a kiosk in a local
shopping mall while the Park Ridge (Illinois) Public Library
has placed a kiosk in their local park district recreation
center.

Local history online

A number of libraries have developed online projects designed to give citizens a greater sense of and connection
to their physical community. The community of Highland

Park, Illinois, has a number of notable historic homes, prompting the Highland Park Public Library to develop "Your Highland Park Home: A Research Guide" *(www.highlandpark.org/homeresearch.html)* which pulls together a number of online resources as an aid to community members. The Fairfax County (Virginia) Public Library provides online access to cemeteries of Fairfax County. This resource allows Web visitors to search through the records of public, commercial, and family burial sites in historic Fairfax County.

The North Suburban Library System in Wheeling, Illinois, has developed the Local History Digitization Project, allowing member libraries to work together to present a comprehensive view of local history. This project provides online tools and resources for member libraries that would like to scan and catalog local history materials. The contents of the collection range from letters from World War II veterans in Park Ridge, Illinois, to selections from the Curt Teich Postcard Collection at the Lake County (Illinois) Museum. The library plays a central role in preserving and displaying local history materials without having to ask community members to give them up to the library or local museum for display.

Community information networks

Aggregating information about the community has long been the role of the public library, both in the physical and virtual world. Libraries were among the first developers and hosts of community information networks designed to serve as one-stop information resources. The community information network is one of the strongest online community-building tools for the local public library. Community information networks allow the library to serve in three important roles:

- Gather information. Community information networks provide libraries with a publishing medium for all of the information on their community that they have traditionally collected. By offering lists of and links to Websites offered by local businesses, service agencies, community clubs, and municipal agencies, the library continues to serve as a central source for information for residents.
- Distribute information. Community information networks give residents the opportunity to provide information about their organizations. Many libraries have long offered space for brochures and flyers from organizations serving their community. By offering Web space on a community information network, the library can expand this role. Community groups are no longer limited by the physical space available in the library, nor are residents seeking information limited by the necessary time constraints imposed by the service hours of the library. Once again, the library can serve in the role of facilitating communication between community members without having to physically mediate the information transactions.
- Reinforce the library's role as the information resource for the community. Finally, by providing a virtual framework for gathering and distributing community information, the library retains and reinforces its role as the source of information in the community. This is, perhaps, the most important reason for a library

to become involved in a community information network. Other groups or corporations can provide the technical infrastructure; however, the library is a known and respected entity in the community. Community members can feel confident that there is someone or something reliable behind the information offered on the community information network. Libraries can also extend their services and hours in the community, essentially providing round-the-clock access to information.

Library-based community information networks

Funded by the Carnegie Library of Pittsburgh (Pennsylvania), the Three Rivers Free-Net *(trfn.clpgh.org)* offers information on the southwestern Pennsylvania area. Three Rivers provides free Web hosting to local not-for-profit groups and government agencies. With links to nearly 1,000 local groups, about half of which are hosted by the community information network, Three Rivers Free-Net provides citizen with access to information on such diverse groups as Aikido of Pittsburgh, Quaker Valley School District, and World War II Veterans of the 4th Ward Pittsburgh.

Three Rivers Free-Net goes beyond offering non-profits the opportunity to have their own Websites. The site prominently publishes a non-profit wish list and provides training to the information providers. The Three Rivers Free-Net also develops and posts content designed to attract users to the site, such as local weather, news, entertainment, and tourism information.

The Columbia Online Information Network, or COIN

(*www.coin.org*), in Columbia, Missouri, follows a slightly different model. COIN is a joint project of the Daniel Boone Regional Library, the County of Boone, and the City of Columbia. COIN also offers affiliate memberships in exchange for a financial contribution to the community information network; affiliate members include a local college, five school districts, and two other city governments. Additionally, as a 501(c)(3) organization, COIN accepts donations from individuals interested in supporting this project.

Like the Three Rivers Free-Net, COIN offers Web hosting services to local government agencies and local community organizations. Visitors can find links to diverse resources such as Mid-Missouri Traditional Dancers, the Columbia Philatelic Society, and the Regional AIDS Interfaith Network. COIN offers links to these Websites by content area or according to geographic location. In addition to Web hosting, COIN provides content features such as a local events calendar and an area called "Public Square" which offers bulletin board and chat services. COIN also links to the EBSCOHost periodicals database; this subscription database is offered at no charge to mid-Missouri citizens accessing the database via COIN.

The NorthStarNet Community Information Network *(www.northstarnet.org)* offers yet another organizational model. NorthStarNet was started by the North Suburban Library System, located in Wheeling, Illinois, and serves libraries in the northern and northwestern suburbs of Chicago. NorthStarNet is a distributed community information network model in which public libraries can choose to participate. Participating libraries set up their own community information pages and recruit and work with local organizations, municipal agencies, and small businesses to set up free Websites on NorthStarNet. Each participating library provides one or more staff members to serve as the local NorthStarNet coordinator. The information providers communicate with the NorthStarNet staff member at their local library. The local NorthStarNet coordinators communicate and network with each other via e-mail–based discussion groups and regular face-to-face meetings. North Suburban Library System—and now the Suburban Library System serving southern and southwestern suburbs of Chicago—provide infrastructure, training, marketing materials, and networking opportunities to their participating libraries. NorthStarNet also offers content designed to attract visitors to the Website overall. The home page links to the NorthStarNet communities and regional resources such as the ChicagoJobs Website. Additionally, NorthStarNet offers residents access to the extensive full-text resources available on the Electric Library information database.

THE PATRON OF THE FUTURE

As the virtual community develops and grows, citizens are making an effort to incorporate these resources and tools into their everyday physical community. However, the generations of children in school now and those to follow will not have to work to blend their physical and virtual communities. The ability to communicate and socialize online is as natural for children and young adults as chatting in the produce section of the grocery store is for their parents and grandparents. The more libraries begin to integrate their online and physical community building, the more likely it is that the patrons of the future will continue to see the library as the information center of their community.

Rolling Meadows (Illinois) Public Library offers such an integrated program in Inkspots, a club for children in fifth through eighth grades. While the Inkspot members meet once a month at the library to work on creative writing and illustration projects, they also have the opportunity to publish their work on the Rolling Meadows Public Library Website *(www.rolling-meadows.lib.il.us/Inkspots main.html)*.

Staff of the Park Ridge (Illinois) Public Library have been working to bring together Web-savvy young adults and civic and business leaders in their community. As part of the Park Ridge Public Library's participation in the NorthStarNet program, their local coordinator has developed a cadre of high school students who are willing to develop Websites for local community groups and small businesses. There are multiple beneficiaries of this program. The students are paid a (very!) reasonable fee for their services. The civic and business groups receive a professionally designed Website at low cost. The library strengthens its role as a key information resource in the community. And, again, after the initial introduction by the library staff, the community members (students and civic leaders) communicate without direct intervention.

Barrington (Illinois) Area Public Library offers an online resource that serves students and teachers in their local schools. At the teacher's request, the Barrington Area Public Library will post assignments or links on the library's home page. Students are able to go online and review information about their assignments while working at the library.

The Fairfax County (Virginia) Public Library focuses on future patrons with the "Connect the Tots" (*www.co. fairfax.va.us/library/tots/menu.htm*) and "Teen Screenz" *(www.co.fairfax.va.us/library/teens/default.htm)* Web areas. "Connect the Tots" offers resources for parents such as a calendar of events and suggested books for children and items of interest to children such as online games, an art gallery, and a "day in the life of a children's librarian" feature. "Teen Screenz" features homework help areas, an art gallery, and Millenium Journal, an online interaction "magazine" for teens.

BENEFITS OF BUILDING COMMUNITY ONLINE

The future benefits of developing online community seem evident; libraries need to adapt to the information-gathering methods of their patrons which are changing as children grow up with the Internet, the World Wide Web, and virtual communities. However, because these technologies are relatively new, there is little concrete data on the value of community-building tools. In fact, one may question whether libraries even have the appropriate tools and methods for evaluating the impact of these services.

By the time of this book's publication, however, we should know more about the benefits of online community-building, thanks to a large study that is currently underway. Funded by the Institute for Museum and Library Studies, "Help-Seeking in an Electronic World" is investigating the role of librarians in assisting users with finding community information over the Internet. Joan Durrance (University of Michigan) and Karen Pettigrew (University of Washington) have conducted an extensive survey of public libraries in North America and are conducting case studies on public library networking systems. (Durrance, 2000: 45)

There is anecdotal evidence of a number of immediate benefits for libraries that develop online community-building tools. Some virtual community tools allow libraries to expand service without keeping the library doors open any longer or hiring additional staff. Being able to extend our expertise is particularly critical when considering the future shortages predicted for professional librarians. By developing tools that enable patrons to help themselves or assist others in gathering reliable information, the library has increased service to their community and strengthened the role of the library in the community. Professor Durrance notes that community information networks serve as "a reminder to community leaders and citizens that librarians are experts" at providing community information." (46)

Additionally, community-building tools help libraries build connections with other organizations within the district and foster the development of new programs. For example, the Ela Area Public Library in Lake Zurich, Illinois, has been involved in the NorthStarNet community information network for four years, with the Hawthorn Woods Police Department as one of their earliest online information providers. Ela Area staff have worked closely with the Hawthorn Woods Police Department to assist them with developing a useful and informative Website. As a result of this relationship, the Web coordinator at the police department and the NorthStarNet library coordinator at Ela started talking about safety issues and the Internet. Together, they developed programs that address child safety and fraud on the Internet. These programs were offered in the physical location of the library (not online) and do not relate directly to their online work together. However, the community information network is the tool that brought these two professionals together and started them thinking about other ways to work together to serve their community. Professor Durrance observes, "Building partnerships with other organizations is a cornerstone to building community."

Finally, these online tools help the library extend their visibility with the traditional—as well as new and unexpected—audiences. As Steve Moskal, director of a public library in Illinois, comments, "It helps us reach out to specific and diverse groups, from young people who would never think of stepping into the library to those who have disabilities and have difficulty traveling" (e-mail communication, March 29, 2000). Online information provides another opportunity for the library to serve as wide an audience as possible.

Community-building tools are a natural extension of the services that libraries have long provided. These tools should not be regarded as fads or extras; rather, they fall into the same category as such long-time library services as walk-up reference service, publicly available meeting rooms, and reader advisory services. Barbara Sugden, Executive Director of the Barrington Area Public Library, concurs, "If the . . . library is to meet its mission of providing information, it must continue to make it easier for district residents to obtain library service instantly without leaving the home or office" (e-mail communication, March 28, 2000).

Libraries wanting to remain the center of their communities should continue looking to some of the examples provided by early pioneers in the arena of online community, such as The Well, and e-business successes, such as Amazon.com. The online community-building techniques employed by these groups can help the library retain and strengthen its role as the key information resource in the community.

RESOURCES

Durrance, Joan. 2000. "Community Information: The Technological Touch." *Library Journal* 125 (February 1): 44–46.

Putnam, Robert. 1995. "Bowling Alone: America's Declining Social Capital." *Journal of Democracy* 6: 65–78. Available: *muse.jhu.edu/demo/journal_of_democracy/v006/putnam.htm.*

Chapter 3

The First Amendment and Library Internet Access

Judith F. Krug

As the Internet seemingly takes over librarians' professional lives, the question arises, often in a humorous way, "What did we do before the Internet?" The truth is that we did the same thing before the advent of the Internet as we have been doing since: namely, bringing people together with the information they need and want. Electronic communication, including the Internet, hasn't changed that traditional role, it hasn't changed what librarians do. It has only changed, to some extent, how they do it. What has not changed at all, however, is librarians' commitment to the concept of intellectual freedom and the place it holds in American librarianship. In short, it is the heart and soul of the profession.

Intellectual freedom is based on the First Amendment to the United States Constitution, particularly, the freedom of the press and freedom of speech clauses. Librarians have interpreted these clauses to mean that every person has the right to hold any belief or idea on any subject and to express those beliefs or ideas in whatever form they consider appropriate. The ability to express an idea or a belief is meaningless, however, unless there is an equal commitment to the right of unrestricted access to information and ideas regardless of the communication medium. Intellectual freedom, then, is the right to express one's ideas and the right of others to be able to read, hear, or view them.

With intellectual freedom as their core value, American librarians have assumed the responsibility to provide, within their collections, ideas and information across the spectrum of social and political thought. The end result is that people can choose what they want to read, or listen to, or look at.

Intellectual freedom is the foundation on which American libraries are built, but equally important, it is also an integral part of the mechanism that allows Americans to govern themselves. The United States is a constitutional republic—a government of the people, by the people, and for the people. But this form of government does not function effectively unless its electorate is enlightened. In short, the electorate, in order to make decisions, must have information available and accessible. And it does—in the nation's libraries.

In today's world, information is available in a variety of formats: books, magazines, films, videos, CD-ROMs, sound recordings, paintings, sculptures, etc. To this mix, electronic communication, specifically the Internet, has been added, leading to the most important and exciting communication revolution since the invention of the printing press. In some key ways, the Internet has changed how librarians bring information together with the people who need it or want it.

Previously, librarians, limited by money and shelf space, selected the items that went into their collections. To a large extent, this still holds true. But it is no longer totally true. The Internet is allowing libraries, for the first time, to make the vast array of ideas and information available to everyone and to permit each library user to act as his or her own selector. This has caused great anguish in certain quarters because some people are convinced that if young people have unfettered access to the Internet, they will be drawn to Websites featuring explicit sex. There does not appear to be evidence to support such beliefs, but no amount of factual evidence or lack thereof has changed the minds of those who so believe.

These same people also find ALA's policies about children and young people to be misguided. These policies urge librarians to provide all users, regardless of age, with the information they need and want. ALA's position has been willfully misinterpreted to mean that children not only do have, but also should have, access to what is termed "inappropriate" library materials. The untruth is spread that librarians actually urge children to look at such material. In this debate, the material that is allegedly "inappropriate" is not clearly defined. Indeed, it sometimes appears as if the definition is: "I don't like it—therefore, it is inappropriate." Such a label has been applied to material as widely varied as the lingerie ads in Victoria's Secret, the images of starlets in bikinis found in *People* magazine and movie star magazines, information about medical matters (for instance, penile implants) and alternative lifestyles of which many people do not approve. There is no distinction made between "pornography," which is an umbrella term for material that people would like to have censored—but, in fact, is protected by the First Amendment and that is definitely legal—and such materials "deemed" to be "obscene," "child pornography," or "harmful to minors," which are not protected and, therefore, are illegal. However, in order to determine whether or not any piece of material can be labeled as "obscene" or "child pornography" or "harmful to minors," it must go through the legal process. These are terms of law, and only legal proceedings can determine if, indeed, a piece of material is illegal.

In many instances, these myths have been translated into legislative proposals. The first such proposal to become law was the Communications Decency Act (CDA), which was signed into law by President Clinton on February 8, 1996, as part of the Telecommunications Reform Act of 1996. The CDA was about keeping "indecent" material from anyone under 18. It said that if "merely" access was provided to the Internet, there was no liability. But if content was provided, the provider risked fines of up to $250,000 and/or up to two years in prison if anyone under 18 was allowed to access "indecent" material over library computers.

The term "indecent," however, was not defined in the legislation. Examples of "indecency" could be found in various court cases, for instance, George Carlin's "7 Dirty Words" monologue was declared "indecent" by the United States Supreme Court; some portions of radio personality Howard Stern's broadcasts were declared "indecent" by a lower court in New York state; and yet another New

York court declared the late Allen Ginsberg's poem "Howl" to be "indecent." But there was no definitive definition that would serve as a guidepost.

In February 1996, two separate lawsuits were filed challenging the constitutionality of the Communications Decency Act. *The American Library Association v the U.S. Department of Justice* was filed after the *American Civil Liberties Union v. Janet Reno* and the cases were consolidated and decided under the title *ACLU v. Reno*. Both legal actions argued three main points:

1. The prohibition of material on the Internet that was "indecent" or "patently offensive" was unconstitutional because these terms were undefined, vague, and over-broad. The suits pointed out that there was no distinction made between material on the Internet appropriate for a five-year-old and that appropriate for a 17-year-old college student. But librarians serve the information needs of the whole community—and 17-year-olds also need "age-appropriate" material. In short, government cannot limit adults (or nearly adults) solely to reading material that is appropriate for children.

2. There are alternate ways for parents to protect their minor children from materials on the Internet they consider inappropriate. Such ways, filters, for instance, would not violate the First Amendment rights of adults and would be more effective than this law. These alternative measures, however, were not considered by Congress, which held no hearings, nor invited any testimony on this issue before passing sweeping legislation.

3. The Internet is *not* a broadcast medium, like television and radio, on which courts have imposed content restrictions on what may be broadcast. Rather, the Internet is more like print—a newspaper, a bookstore, a library—because the audience is not captive. Each member of the audience has control over what he or she can access, each has a choice. Accordingly, the Internet deserves the same First Amendment protection as books and newspapers, not the lesser protection granted to the broadcast medium.

In June 1996, a lower court declared the CDA unconstitutional. The government appealed, and on June 26, 1997, by a 9–0 vote, the United States Supreme Court declared the Communications Decency Act unconstitutional. The High Court said:

1. Adults cannot be limited in their reading material to only that which is suitable for children.
2. There are alternate means, such as filters for parents to use at home, to protect their children.
3. The Internet is more like the print medium than like the broadcast medium, and deserves the same First Amendment protection enjoyed by print. The Court, in fact, went a step further and said electronic communications may be entitled to even more First Amendment protection than print!

ALA's lawyer called the decision "the birth certificate of the Internet." It set the standard by which all future regulation of cyberspace communications would be judged by all other U.S. courts. By a unanimous Supreme Court decision, the freedom of expression on the Internet and access to that expression is protected in the United States. Nevertheless, that has not stopped Congress, state legislatures, and many local governments from spending vast amounts of time trying to figure out how to get around it and implement what some consider to be the solution to "bad stuff" on the Internet—namely, filters.

Contrary to popular belief, the American Library Association is not against filters. Indeed, ALA believes filters are appropriate devices for parents to use at home with their children. When they are used at home, parents can program them according to their value system and the principles they wish to instill in their children. But while the American Library Association believes that filters can be used by parents at home, ALA does not believe filters are appropriate for public institutions. There are several reasons for this:

- Libraries are publicly supported governmental institutions and as such, are subject to the First Amendment. The First Amendment forbids government-funded libraries from restricting information based on viewpoint or content.
- Libraries are places of inclusion rather than exclusion. Current blocking/filtering software prevents access not only to what some may consider to be "objectionable" material, but also to information protected by the First Amendment. The result is that legal and valuable information inevitably is blocked. For instance, sites that have been blocked by popular commercial blocking/filtering products include those on breast cancer, AIDS, women's rights, animal rights, the American

Association of University Women, all groups known as "associations," the FBI, eBay, golfer Fred Couples, and the Mars exploration, which has the URL of MARSEXPL.

- Most filter manufacturers consider their blockages to be proprietary information and, therefore, will not reveal what is being blocked or how it is being blocked.
- Software developers are making selection decisions for communities based on their bias of beliefs, not the norms or values of the particular communities.
- Filters cannot and do not block all of the material that many prefer not be accessible to children. Even the filtering manufacturers admit it is impossible to block all undesirable material. The Web is too vast and changes too quickly for filters to be effective. While research figures have varied widely, there is little debate that filters are not as effective as originally hoped. More importantly for librarians, filters eliminate up to 40 percent of sites that contain bona fide, valuable, useful information. The truth is, filters are merely mechanical devices and mechanical devices have no judgmental capabilities or decision making abilities. They are "things!"

For all of these reasons, then, filters are not appropriate for libraries.

When all is said and done, how a library handles the Internet is a local decision. ALA's policies encourage libraries to provide open access to all library users. ALA believes that education in the use of library resources, including the Internet, is a much better solution to connecting children and the Internet than is filtering.

There are strategies available for managing the Internet in accordance with the First Amendment. They include:

- Internet Use policies that define the level of Web access based on age. Most libraries require young children to be accompanied by a parent or guardian.
- Codes of conduct that define appropriate use of library computers and the Internet (e.g., no participation in illegal activities such as child pornography or gambling).
- Internet training classes for children and parents to teach them how to do an online search and other techniques that can ensure a positive online experience.
- Links to pre-selected sites such as the American Library Association's 700+ Great Sites for Kids and search engines specially designed for children such as KidsClick! Or AOL's NetFind for Kids.
- Privacy screens on workstations.
- Time limits and other rules for computer use in keeping with the library's mission statement and customer service practices.

Librarians' main responsibility is to bring people together with the information they need or want. The format in which that information appears has little bearing on that responsibility, as does the age of the user of the information. In fact, Article 5 of the Library Bill of Rights states: "A person's right to use the library should not be denied or abridged because of origin, age, background, or views." To put it bluntly, the librarian's role never has been, is not currently, and will not be in the future to keep people from the information they need and want. If the

United States is to continue to be a nation of self-governors, the people must have available and accessible the information they need to make decisions.

James Madison said it the best almost 200 years ago: "A popular Government, without popular information, or the means of acquiring it, is but a prologue to a farce or a tragedy; or, perhaps, both. Knowledge will forever govern ignorance and a people who mean to be their own governors must arm themselves with the power knowledge gives" (Symons and Reed, 1999).

RESOURCES

Symons, Ann and Sally Gardner Reed. 1999. *Speaking Out! Voice in Celebration of Intellectual Freedom.* Chicago: American Library Association: 44.

Chapter 4

Working with Parents to Manage the Internet Controversy

Ann K. Symons

Every year nearly four million kids are born in the United States—white, black, Hispanic, Native American, Asian, and more. Most are wanted, some are not. The majority of kids are loved and treasured, others are abused. Some are rich, others are poor. Just as kids come in all sizes and colors, so do parents. The number of traditional "two-parent" families has declined significantly. We see families with one mom, or one dad, two moms, two dads, blended families, grandparents as primary caregivers, and almost any combination you can imagine. Just about every parent, young or old, has hopes and dreams that their child will grow up to be a productive citizen, that they will be able to read, make decisions, be critical thinkers, and in today's jargon, be information literate.

Today's kids all have one thing in common: they were born and live in a digital age. Their parents did not. In the year 2000, in the United States, there were almost 20 million kids under the age of five, over 36 million kids ages 3–13, and almost 16 million teenagers, ages 14–17. Technology is not an option in the lives of kids today. Whether it is a house that manages itself with technology, a computer in every room, a cell phone for every member of the family, or a VCR and microwave, digital technology is a part of all of our lives—at home, at school, and at work. Children born about 2000 won't remember a world without the Internet, e-mail, and the World Wide Web. Parents are learning at different rates to cope with the societal changes the Internet has brought.

Growing up, kids will get their values from their parents, from caregivers, religious institutions, schools—and they will remain minors in their parents' care until they are 18 years old.

It is natural that parents want to protect their children from illness, from hurt, from abuse, from anything that affects their health and safety. Protecting children often includes protection from ideas parents don't agree with and from information they consider inappropriate for their children. Sex and sexually explicit images is not the only thing parents today worry about in the online world. Some parents consider a whole raft of online material to be inappropriate, including violence, hate speech, games, and drugs. My parents didn't worry about what I might see on the Internet, whether or not I would agree to meet somebody I met in a "chat room," whether or not I would give out my name, address, and phone number to a digital stranger, whether I would be harassed by e-mail messages urging me to visit an inappropriate Website or whether I would buy things online with my parents' credit cards without permission.

In a recent research study done by the Annenberg Public Policy Center, "The Internet and the Family: The View from Parents, The View from the Press," Dr. Joseph Turow found that "The majority of American parents with computers at home juggle the dream and the nightmare of the Internet at the same time. Most parents with online connections at home are deeply fearful about the Web's influence on their children" (Turow, 1999). Reflecting compound fears, most of the parents surveyed feel their children are growing up in a digital age and if they don't have the Internet somehow they will be at a disadvantage in school and, eventually, the job market. More are concerned that their kids will see sexually explicit materials or give personal information to strangers.

Today we hear about the Internet controversy everywhere, and nowhere is that controversy more pronounced than in our schools and our public libraries. Parents want to protect their children, organizations want to protect society from sin, corruption, and sex. Legislators want votes. Nobody seems content to deal with only their children. Protecting other people's children has become a national pastime.

There is no Internet controversy at home, or if there is, it is between parent and child. Parents with computers at home set rules, they have the final say, they can choose to control what their kids see or don't see. They can use a variety of strategies that work for their family to keep their kids safe on the Internet. Ensuring a child's safety online works best when a parent is with a child; however, for families without computers at home, libraries are the number one access point to get online.

Parents want the same rules to apply when they can't be with their child, when their child is at school or at the public library. And yet public institutions are not homes. Expecting parental supervision at all times is not going to happen and is not going to solve the problem. Technology is not the problem nor is it the sole answer to protecting children.

Fact: we have a controversy we need to manage in our libraries—public, school and less so academic. The controversy, like many others, is evident when values conflict. In this case the conflict is between the value of open access to information for all and the need to protect children. Further, we set up a nearly impossible situation when we defend both children's rights to open access and the parents' rights to guide their children's use, but then we often don't help parents in ways they feel they would like to be helped.

We, as librarians, often think about how free access to books, ideas, and information undergirds our democracy. We know that each day millions of people of all ages and backgrounds walk into libraries expecting to find and receive information on almost every conceivable topic free of charge. We don't make judgements about what people read, hear, or view. We connect them with the information they need to live, work, and learn in school or at home.

"Libraries: An American Value," an ALA document, states in part:

We defend the constitutional rights of all individuals,

including children and teenagers, to use the library's resources and services AND We affirm the responsibility and the right of all parents and guardians to guide their own children's use of the library and its resources and services.

In any conflict of values there is no winning side. The key is to understand the conflict and put in place a strategy that involves the entire library community, and particularly librarians who serve youth. In any conflict of values there are strong pressures and the stakes are high. The battle over protecting kids through filters vs. freedom of speech takes place in our courts, legislatures, communities, elections, and our libraries.

Some controversies end up in court, such as in Virginia, where a citizen's group called Mainstream Loudoun sued the Loudoun County Public Library to remove filters, or in California, where a mother wanting filters sued the Livermore Public Library because it did not filter access. Most controversies, however, are played out in the political arena surrounded by media coverage.

The answer is not to avoid challenges, criticism, or controversy. The answer is to work with your community and to put your "Parent Plan in place." Librarians care about children. Many of us are parents. Some of us have dedicated our professional lives to serving children. We know there is more than one way to protect children.

Library technology today could be programmed—and in some cases it is—to carry out the wishes of each and every individual parent. Solving the Internet problem with technology, including filtering software, however, is not the answer.

Addressing the issue of "child safety on the Internet" for the library community is an education issue for trustees, parents, librarians, decision makers, and children. The opportunity to help parents learn how to guide their children in using the Internet is one of the most exciting opportunities we have today. We all want the same thing—for kids to have a safe, educational, and rewarding experience online.

GUIDANCE

How do we take advantage of this opportunity and what do we, as librarians, need to do? As we start down a road which begins with library policy and ends with a public education and advocacy campaign, remember that you are not beginning at zero. Librarians have always been willing to share.

Before we get to the Parent Plan, let's review what we know—or should know—about kids of various ages.

Kids

Begin with the basics: if you can't read you can't use the Internet. Yes, there are a few Websites designed for toddlers, but, for the most part, very young children are not interested in the Internet and they certainly aren't using it alone. Children mature and learn at different rates. The U.S. Department of Education has set a goal that all kids read independently by the end of the third grade. Being able to read is only one part of the equation. We must not only teach children to read but to differentiate between useful and valuable information and content that is not useful or offensive to their family values.

Walter Minkel, technology editor of *School Library Journal*, recently wrote, "Because it [the Web] requires fairly sophisticated print and visual literacy skills, the web is not developmentally appropriate for kids to use alone until they are third graders at minimum." He further went on to suggest that as librarians we should be spending our energies "connecting . . . parents and caregivers to web resources they can use" (Minkel, 2000).

Parents often ask, "When is my child ready to use a computer?" Is the question when is my child ready to use the Internet, or when is my child ready to use a computer? There are many CD-ROM programs designed for pre-schoolers and young children that do not require the same level of reading and critical thinking skills that the Internet does.

The Children's Partnership, in conjunction with the National Urban League and the Parent Teacher Association (PTA), have published a second edition of their well-received *The Parents' Guide to the Information Superhighway; Rules and Tools for Families Online* (Children's Partnership, 2000). An excellent resource for any parent, the Guide outlines common sense, age-appropriate guidelines for computer use. Keeping in mind that children mature both physically and emotionally at different rates, parents know their children best. There are no fixed points at which a child must exhibit certain skills. Often, parenting magazines will review computer programs and Websites for children. Having a bibliography of the best articles regarding online experiences, rules, and software available for parents is what we, as librarians, do best—

connecting people with the information they need. Parental involvement is very important as young children begin to use computers. It is also the time to begin establishing rules. Some library policies require that parents use the computer with their young children.

By the time children are approaching the age of eight, they often are beginning to go online at school with supervision and learning specific skills as part of the technology curriculum, at home with parents, and at the library with the help of parents and librarians. The American Library Association's "700+ Great Sites for Kids" is a link that almost all libraries with kids pages use (ALA, 1997).

ParenTech, a partnership of Ameritech and the North Central Regional Education Laboratory, has published both in print and online an extensive package of materials for parenting in the digital age designed for parents of middle-school–age children and young adults.

The teen years are tough. Kids want to explore widely and that extends to such Internet explorations as chat rooms. It is just as important for parents to work with their teenagers as it is with younger children. Obviously, sitting with them as they go online is not generally the answer at this age. Many of the parents' tips such as rules—particularly for chat rooms—and consequences apply now more than ever. The job of the parent is to decide what is acceptable and what is not acceptable for their children and to communicate that message to the child. It is also the job of the parent to protect their child by knowing what the right answer is when children are harassed or get into uncomfortable situations, be it with peers or with strangers.

The Internet controversy often focuses on young children. As "children" near the age of maturity, the law grants them more First Amendment rights than it does young children. Teenagers make up a particularly interesting group. They often have less parental supervision and more freedom to come and go both in the real and the virtual world. Rebecca Dill, interviewed as a 17-year-old for Mary Motley Kalegis's book *Seen and Heard; Teenagers Talk about Their Lives*, says, "As far as sex is concerned, teenagers are full of hormones and curiosity, so it's crazy to try and deny us access to information. The more we know, the more informed decision we can make. Ignorance and fear just result in unplanned pregnancy or sexually transmitted disease" (Kalegis, 1998).

Shortly after the tragic shootings in Littleton, Colorado, *Newsweek* (May 10, 1999) carried a cover story about teens. Some of the facts their researchers found are useful as librarians plan library services for teens. Teens today comprise 10 percent of the U.S. population and most of them have working parents. Among single mothers of teens, 70 percent work compared to 60 percent of both parents working, which means that a lot of teens are unsupervised after school. By 2003, 70 percent of all teens will go online. Today slightly less than 60 percent of teens are online (Leland, 1999). When they get there, what do they do? The majority of teens do e-mail and searching. Music sites, research, games, TV and movie sites, chat rooms, their own Web pages, a predictable mix of typical teenage interests.

The same issue of *Newsweek* cited a survey of parents that shows what parents are doing with their kids while they are online.

Activity	Age 11–15	Age 16–18
Sit with them while online	38%	9%
Kids can log on only with an adult	34%	5%
Mainly use for online games	28%	15%
Limit hours for kids use	47%	21%
Know which Websites kids can visit	68%	43%
Kids are online whenever they want	54%	75%
Use the Net more than watch TV	19%	22%

As older teenagers, the majority of kids are online whenever they want; very few parents sit with their teen while they go online—and most of them worry. Leland went on to write, "with as many as 11 million teenagers now online, more and more of adolescent life is taking place in a landscape that is inaccessible to many parents" (Leland, 1999). *Newsweek* also reported a poll of Americans regarding teenagers and the Internet, finding that "47 percent of Americans say very few parents really know what their teens are up to; 60 percent say the government should restrict access to some Internet material." And when you don't know what teens are up to, one of the things they are doing is spending money online—their parents' money. In 1999, teens' spending online doubled and it is expected to double again in 2000, according to *Yahoo! Internet Life* ("Generation Wired," 2000). Teens are also turning to the Web to ask questions they don't feel comfortable asking their parents. They keep in contact with friends and they use the Web as a reflection of their interests.

THE PARENT PLAN

Every day, millions of children and young adults use libraries in their schools and local communities. The Internet offers kids rich resource for information and communication, educational tools, and sites that are fun and entertaining. More than ten million children use the Internet every day. One search goes wrong in your community and all of a sudden parents, politicians, and the media are asking for restrictions on access. The time to manage the Internet controversy in your library is not when you have a community controversy on your hand, but long before. The key to success is to manage the Internet. Parents play a big role in how successful your library will be.

Instead of talking about what we are not doing, we need to focus on positive action. Educating parents and other adults who work with kids is a big part of the answer to keeping kids safe on the Internet. Libraries are one of the few institutions that offer training for parents

The "Parent Plan" is a combination of best library practice, community needs, common sense, library values, hard work, setting goals to reach out to parents, and stretching your services to highlight the key role parents play in the lives of their children. Courtesy, calmness, and reassurance to parents should underlie the plan. Make sure that you know what parents' options are for "protecting their child" at home, at school, and at the library. Make sure that parents know what their options are; they may be different in each situation. If your community's school district is filtering and your public library is not, how is this going to play out in the community?

Software filters are often seen as a quick fix, especially

by politicians and others not familiar with the Internet and how it works. One of the concerns about filters is that they can give parents a false sense that their children are protected when, in fact, they aren't. Of the millions of sites on the Internet, there are some all of us would agree are undesirable for children. We need to plan in which media we will describe the Internet in all its complexity, both the good and the bad, and help educate parents about the support available to them from schools, libraries, and other institutions. And we need legislators who will take the time to learn about the Internet and craft thoughtful solutions, not rush to judgment.

The absolute best way to protect children when it comes to the Internet—or just about anything else—is for parents to supervise their children, to teach them basic safety rules and how to make positive choices. This means taking a few precautions, using common sense, and practicing some good old fashioned family values, like taking responsibility for our own children and teaching them to live responsibly. As the tragic events in Littleton, Colorado, show, that goes for older as well as younger children.

The plan, which is nothing more than a public education and advocacy plan, includes the following components:

- Key messages
- Internet access policies in place approved by your governing board
- Internal and external scan of your resources
- Community discussion
- Tips for parents
- Library Websites for kids

- Library Websites for parents
- A plan to teach kids to use the Internet
- A plan to teach kids and their parents together
- A plan to contain offensive viewing through the use of privacy screens, terminal placement, or "drop-in" terminals
- Emphasis on parental responsibility for what kids see
- Advice on best practices shared with others on listservs such as PUBLIB and LM-Net, at state and national conferences such as PLA and ALA
- Knowledge of your media market and how you will use it to benefit the library

A school district is more likely to already have in place many mechanisms for reaching parents. Differing from public libraries, school districts also have an education plan, called curriculum, in place. The key to any good plan in public libraries or schools are your core messages and how you intend to put them into place. Image is everything and superior graphics make a difference. Libraries serve all families who live in a community. It is up to each family to figure out what they want their children to see and to set rules.

Let us examine in more detail each of the components of the Parent Plan.

Key messages

No plan is effective without a clear idea of what you want to communicate. Some key messages you might consider:

- Librarians: partners with parents

- Libraries are part of the solution to how families deal with the Internet
- Librarians help by pointing kids and their parents to good and useful information
- Librarians help parents assess the value and reliability of information on the Internet
- Our goal is for every child to have a safe and rewarding experience online
- The Internet is neither good nor evil—it is a tool to communicate, to publish, and to find information, one that we as a society are still learning to use.

Internet access policies

Today, about three-fourths of all public libraries provide public access to the Internet. Much has been written in the literature about the needs to have library policy in place and to have those policies approved by the library's governing body, be it the trustees of the library, the school board of a local school district, or the governing authority of an academic institution. In any discussion regarding community access to the Internet it should always be stressed that policy decisions are made at the local level, keeping in mind that libraries are publicly funded government agencies and have a responsibility to uphold public access to legal information as defined by the Constitution, federal, state, and local laws.

Virtually every library has an Internet use policy that protects both children and public access to useful information. Most libraries post their Internet policy on their Website. Not all policies will be the same. Local libraries adopt their own policies according to the needs, values, and standards of the community. Some policies require a "guardian" signature to use the Internet. Some require parents to be present when children use the Internet. Some set time limits. Some revoke Internet privileges for viewing materials that are inappropriate or offensive to others. Some link computers in children's rooms only to pre-selected sites. Some use filters. Some place age restrictions on use of the library by children alone; others say that parents must use the Internet with their children who are under a certain age.

Your existing resources

What are your resources for parents and kids? What do you have in place now? Have you compared it to what other libraries are doing? How do you rate? What do you need to do and how are you going to measure success? Is your library doing training for the public now? When can you start? Who can you partner with in your community? What percentage of your community has computers in the home? Who are you trying to reach? An environmental scan often will give you and parents information that you can put to use in setting goals and strategies for a successful Parent Plan.

Community discussion

Do you do this before or after controversy erupts? You would have to be almost dead today to not know that there are things on the Internet that many parents do not want their children to see. Is putting policies with normal opportunities for public discussion enough? If you think so, then ask yourself what community discussion looks like when the American Family Association walks in your door and objects to children seeing pornography in the library. Just as there is no one policy solution for children's access issues for every community, there is no single community discussion model involving parents that fits every community.

The key to any discussion is to pay careful attention. Who's doing the talking? Is it parents, politicians, your board of trustees, an organized group with a concern to express? Ask yourself—who are you hearing from? Is it a vocal minority? Is it the majority of your community? Everyone wants to "protect children," but what does that really mean? What does it mean in law? What does it mean in public policy? What does it mean in public libraries?

As the Santa Clara County (California) Public Library found out, the solution is not about debating Internet filtering but about managing the Internet in their library community. That library board asked themselves that question during a controversy over library policy. The library hired the Markkula Center for Applied Ethics, an ethics center affiliated with Santa Clara University, to work with their community on values conflicts. "Markkula's charge was to provide a neutral place for all players to express their opinions. They also were to offer a process to the Board for making an ethical and thoughtful decision that honored the concerns of everyone. Markkula was not charged to recommend a solution but to focus on an ethical process." Ultimately, the Santa Clara County Public Library board decided to filter computers in the children's rooms, but children could use unfiltered computers elsewhere in the library. (See Chapter 10 for the full Santa Clara County case history.)

Controlling public discussion during a controversy is often difficult. It often leads to an airing of all of the issues and you have to trust your community to make the right decisions. When egregious decisions are made, you can expect the First Amendment community in some form to stop on your door step with a message—or a lawsuit.

Tips for parents

First, make the time to learn about the Internet and how it works. The more you know and understand this medium the less frightening it will be. Your public or school library can offer classes and materials to help parents guide their children.

How can parents reassure themselves that their children are protected from harmful material both at home and in the library? Consider the following strategies.

- Be involved: spend time with your kids.
- Set a goal of building your technical skills.
- Buy a computer for the family if you can afford one; if not, know where in your community you can access the Internet for free.
- Assess your needs: for what purposes do you want to use the Internet at home? E-mail, chat, Web browsing, games?
- Put your home computer in a family area such as the family room, den, kitchen, where families have more opportunities to discuss what's coming into the house. Be there!
- Consider monitoring kids' use: Web browsers store records of what sites users visit in a history file. Par-

ents can monitor their kids' activities with just elementary computer savvy.

- Have your kids teach you about the Internet.
- Talk with your kids, express genuine interest in what they are doing.
- Set time limits for your kids online and monitor them, just as you would television.
- Ask your child to use a computer in a specific area at the library.
- Set rules. The Annenberg report shows that parents are already setting rules as one of the methods to protect their kids online. Why? Because they know it works. We don't let children play in the street. Neither should we let them play unsupervised on the Internet. Children should be taught not to give their names to strangers on- or offline. There are lots of other common-sense tips that can ensure children have a positive experience online. Your family rules should reflect the age of the child. If your rules say that your child can't go online without you, follow them.
- Teach your children values and guidelines to use in selecting what they read and view. Let them know what subjects and Websites are off limits and explain why. Introduce your child to the children's librarian and encourage him/her to ask for help when seeking information on the Internet.
- Whether at home or in the library, stay involved with your kids online.
- If you use filtering software at home, be aware that useful information will be blocked and not all "bad" information will be filtered.
- Learn about the Internet and how it works.

- Learn about child-safe search engines.
- Don't let your child surf alone without setting rules.
- Ask librarians for help; encourage your child to ask for help.
- Discuss with your kids your family's privacy policy regarding monitoring computer records.
- Teach responsible digital citizenship.

Library Websites for kids

Every library that offers Internet access to the public should have a "kids' page." There is too much unorganized information out there for kids to waste their time and energy trying to find something appropriate for their interest and age level. This is an area where librarians have always excelled—selecting the best of the best for any age group. If you do not have the resources to have an extensive page for kids, link to some of the best kids' pages which have been done by librarians. The ALA's "700+ Great Websites for Kids" is one example. Don't forget a teen page. It is just as important to offer excellent resources for teens as well. ALA's "Teen Hoopla" is one page that fits this bill. Be creative. Learn to be a Webmaster; it's a skill that is going to be with us, as librarians, for a long time.

Library Websites for parents

It is more unusual to find a Web page specifically for parents than it is to have a page for kids. Libraries with pages for parents often link them from their kids' page! Take another look at your library's page. You are missing an opportunity if there is not a link to information for parents from your homepage. The majority of libraries have no specific information for parents. It is not hard to gather several great resources and add them as a service to parents. For good examples of parent Websites, visit the home pages of the Los Angeles Public Library (*www.lapl.org/ kidsweb/4adultswhocareaboutkids-Op.html*), and the Wilton (Connecticut) Public Library (*www.wiltonlibrary. org*).

Teach kids to use the Internet, teach them with their parents, teach adults to use the Internet

One of the most popular services you can offer your community is classes on how to use the Internet. We often assume that because we are Web-savvy, e-mail–savvy and have been using the Internet for "years" to find information, that everyone shares our skills. They do not! Librarians, because of the nature of our profession, and our focus on access to information in many formats, are well suited to teach our skills to children and adults. If you don't have the resources to offer classes in a "lab situation," look around your community and see who does have training facilities. Often, school district computers labs can be used in the evening. Partnering with a school district to teach parents and kids together is a way to help lessen parents' fears about the Websites they think "pop up" on the screen. Tie in training opportunities with local companies who have training facilities The Wilton Public Library offers classes for both adults and adults with kids. They charge ten dollars per session and the proceeds go directly into providing more technology in the library.

Teach In is targeted at a specific time of the year. Tool

kits for parents, Internet safety videos (done by local kids), a cyber line for people to get answers, specific classes dealing with child-safe search engines, children's privacy issues, examples of software filtering, are all ways to enhance the educational component of your teaching.

Have a speaker's bureau to provide programs for schools, government, and civic organizations. Explore role-playing for parents and add some interaction to reach out to parents. Present them real life situations: "What would you do if . . ." and ask them to do some role playing as part of your training. Use these opportunities to dispel myths and convey facts. Establish a parent tech discussion group. Offer online training for families via your Website, (i.e., through Families Connect, described more fully below). The important thing is to make your training a regular ongoing part of the library—it is a two-way channel of communication with the community where you can deliver your message and listen to parental concerns.

One way to learn how to use the Internet is to sign up for a free online course called "Internet Families Connect." This is a technology initiative of the American Association of School Librarians, a division of the American Library Association. The course is described on the AASL Website (*www.ala.org/ICONN/familiesconnect.html*) as follows:

> Free online course introduces families to the Internet. FamiliesConnect, the parent/extended family component of the American Association of School Librarians' (AASL) ICONnect technology initiative, offers a free online course for families. "FamiliesConnect: An Introduction to the Internet," is a five lesson course designed to help parents, grandparents, and other

extended family members learn about the Internet and how to use it with children and their information needs. Anyone with Internet access and a basic understanding of e-mail can register for the course.

The first lesson provides a brief history of the Internet, defines terms related to Internet use, and describes 12 ways families can use the Internet together including making travel plans and visiting virtual museums. The second lesson is an overview of ways to find information on the Internet including using a variety of search tools, homework sites, ICONnect's KidsConnect service and subscription-based services such as online encyclopedias. E-mail and the way it has changed the way people communicate is the topic of the third lesson. The fourth lesson addresses privacy concerns, child safety, the use of the Internet in schools and the pros and cons of home Internet filtering programs. The fifth and final lesson covers criteria for evaluating Websites, intellectual property rights and citing information found on the Internet.

Each lesson features recommended sites related to its topic that will be accessible via a Web page created specifically for the course. Recommendations for books and other materials for more in-depth information are also included in the lessons.

Limit offensive viewing through the use of privacy screens, terminal placement, "drop-in" terminals

Parents often object to having their kids inadvertently see what other library patrons are viewing. We know from recent court cases that libraries cannot restrict adults from looking at material that is constitutionally protected. Some of that material is sexually explicit. If you have concerns or parents have raised issues with the library director or board, one of the ways to manage your Internet resources is by taking steps to ensure that terminals have privacy screens or are placed in such a way that inadvertent viewing is not the norm.

Place the responsibility for what kids see on parents

There is no other way to say this—and libraries have been saying it for years—a parent or guardian and only that parent or guardian gets to decide what his or her child sees, hears, views, and reads. Not your child, not my child— their own children. It is also not the responsibility of the library staff to carry out parents' wishes regarding what they see. Technology has definitely made it possible for libraries to use the technology to carry out parent wishes and some libraries have used this option to lessen controversy in their communities. Parental signature required to use the Internet for children under 18 is becoming more common. Requiring a parent to choose between filtered and unfiltered access for their child is another possible automated solution. While these solutions are possible it will ultimately be the courts which tell us whether they are unconstitutional. Imagine being $17^{1}/_{2}$ and not having access at the library at all, or only filtered access. I'd probably spend my earned money—if I worked—and go to a cybercafe.

Libraries have used different strategies for conveying this important message to kids. The Sno-Isle Regional Library has a positively worded statement available to parents when they come to the library (*www.sno-isle.org/visitors/*).

SHARE BEST PRACTICES

We all learn from each other. Sharing what we do best in our communities is on listservs such as PUBLIB, LM-NET, and at state and national conferences such as PLA and ALA. Write about what you are doing and submit your article to *American Libraries*, *School Library Journal*, *Library Journal* or any of the many state publications.

WORK WITH THE MEDIA

Know your media market and how you will use it to benefit the library. If your library has a public information officer, use the expertise of that person and the office. "I don't have time for your plan" is probably not an option if you consider the amount of time often spent during a crisis. Journalists often place the burden of dealing with the Web on parents without telling them where they can get help. The press may portray parents facing the Web virtually alone, but we know there are libraries and librarians in communities across America who can and are helping parents and kids become Web-savvy. We need to get the media to tell our story.

Also consider the following points when developing your media plan:

- Figure out what your plan is for dispelling the image of the sexual predator stalking children at the library, and the image of children sitting around looking at

sexually explicit images.
- Know what your key message is for every media contact (i.e., "We are there to help answer parents' questions," "We all want to protect children," etc.).
- Tie in media attention to parents with an existing campaign, i.e., Library Card Sign Up Month. Share existing information materials with the press.
- Plan your releases for newspapers, television, radio, periodicals, and electronic publication. Make sure all your press releases are on your Website. Above all, be prepared for any community crisis involving the library, parents, and Internet access.

QUESTIONS PARENTS ASK

Always be prepared for a parent to come in and ask questions. Many parents are not as technologically proficient as their kids. Most are genuinely interested and concerned. Be parent-savvy and always be prepared to answer the following questions. You may want to write out your answers and place them on your parent Website as Frequently Asked Questions (FAQ).

General questions parents might ask
- Where is the most likely place for my child to encounter a stalker?
- What if I have never used a computer before?
- What age should my child be before they begin using a computer?
- Where do I find safety tips?

- How can I tell a good Website from a bad one. What "criteria" should I use?
- If I want to monitor what my kids see, how do I do that?
- What should I tell my kids to do when they accidentally get someplace they shouldn't be?
- What do I need to know about online shopping?
- Are Websites collecting information about my children from the library (or home)?
- What are cookies?
- What does my family need to know about Internet privacy?
- What do you know about Internet privacy?

Questions parents might ask of their public library

- Is the library filtering?
- What is being blocked?
- What guarantee do you have that my child won't see anything offensive?
- Can my child use a computer that isn't filtered?
- May I have a demonstration?
- How does this work?
- Who decides what young people can or cannot see?
- I have a 16-year-old, a 12-year-old and a 7-year-old. Does the same filter work for all of them?
- What do I have to sign for my child to use the Internet?
- Is there free access in our community?
- Is there an inexpensive cybercafé around here where I could try things out?

Questions particular to school districts

- May I see the school district's technology plan?
- Are there state or district technology standards that say what a child should learn and when?
- Technology curriculum; how is it integrated into other curricula?
- May I see the school district's Internet access policy?
- What are the consequences for my child misusing the Internet?
- Is the library filtering?
- What is being blocked?
- What guarantee do you have that my child won't see anything offensive?
- Can my child use a computer that isn't filtered?
- May I have a demonstration?
- Do you have a permission form to put my child's work on the Web?
- Do you have a permission form to put my child's picture on the Web?
- Am I assured that you will not put my child's name, address, and phone number on the Web?
- What opportunities are there for parent involvement in the school's or district's technology planning efforts?
- Is there a tech night in my child's school? Can I help?
- What parent volunteer opportunities are there involving technology?

CONCLUSION

If our children are to succeed as adults, they must learn to make good judgments about the information they encounter, both positive and negative. Teaching and trusting children to make good decisions about where they go and what they do is what being a parent is all about. Fortunately, there are librarians, teachers, and others to help. For many children, schools and public libraries may be the only places they may go to have access to the same online world that their peers have at home. Public and school libraries are playing a critical role in closing the gap between the information-rich and the information-poor. Librarians were among the first to recognize the importance of equity on the information superhighway.

The freedom to select for ourselves and our children what we read, hear, and view is one of the most precious rights in a democracy. Each day, millions of people of all ages and backgrounds walk into libraries expecting to find and receive information on almost any conceivable topic free of charge, no questions asked. Many parents will ask no questions, but many will want to know everything about your library's services. Be prepared. Work your plan! What librarians do and have always done is to select, organize, evaluate, and categorize information to make it easy to find and use. Make your Parent Plan work by doing what we have always done—reaching out to the communities we want to target.

RESOURCES

Access, Internet, and Public Libraries: A Report to the Santa Clara County Libraries [Online]. Available: *www.scu.edu/SCU/Centers/Ethics/practicing/focusareas/technology/libraryaccess/*.

American Association of School Librarians. 1998. ICONnect [Website]. Available: *www.ala.org/ICONN/*. (Online classes for parents, librarians, teachers, and others in how to use the Internet as an Educational Resource.)

American Library Association. *Libraries and the Internet Toolkit: Tips and Guidance for Managing and Communicating About the Internet* [Online]. Available: *www.ala.org/internettoolkit/index.html*. [February 2000].

American Library Association. *700+ Great Sites for Kids* [Online]. Available: *www.ala.org/parentspage/greatsites/amazing.html* [1997].

American Library Association. *Teen Hoopla: An Internet Guide for Teens* [Online]. Available: *www.ala.org/teenhoopla*. (Links to resources of special interest to teens. This site is provided by the Young Adult Library Services Association, a division of the American Library Association.)

Children's Partnership and the National PTA and the National Urban League. *The Parents' Guide to the Information Superhighway; Rules and Tools for Families,* 2nd edition [Online]. Available: *www.childrenspartnership.org* (May 1998).

Direct Marketing Association. *Get Cyber Savvy A Family Guide* [Online]. Available: *www.the-dma.org*.

"Generation Wired: What are teens up to online? It's probably not what you think." *Yahoo! Internet Life* (March 2000): 150.

GetNetWise [Website]. Available: *www.getnetwise.org/.* (GetNetWise is a resource for families and caregivers to help kids have safe, educational, and entertaining online experiences.)

Kalegis, Mary Motley. 1998. *Seen and Heard: Teenagers Talk About Their Lives.* New York: Steward, Tabor & Chang.

Katz, John. "The Rights of Kids in the Digital Age." *Wired,* July 1997.

KidsConnect [Website]. Available: *www.ala.org/ICON/ AskKC.html.* (An online question-and-answer service for students operated by the American Association of School Librarians, a division of the American Library Association, in partnership with the Information Institute of Syracuse University.)

Kids Page of the Carnegie Library of Pittsburgh [Online]. Available: *www.clgh.org/kidspage.*

Leland, John. "The Secret Life of Teens," *Newsweek,* May 10, 1999: 45–50.

Los Angeles Public Library. *For Adults Who Care about Kids* [Online] Available: *www.lapl.org/kidsweb/ 4adultswhocareaboutkids-Op.html.*

Minkel, Walter. "Young Children AND the Web: A Boolean Match, or NOT?" In: *Library Journal Net Connect; a Librarian's Link to the Internet,* a supplement to *Library Journal* 125 (January 2000): 10–11.

Monroe County Public Library, Bloomington [Website]. Available: *www.monroe.lib.in.us/children/childrens_ dept.html.*

National Center for Missing and Exploited Children. 1998. *Child Safety on the Information Highway* [Online]. Available: *www.missingkids.com.*

ParenTech; parenting in a Digital Age [Website]. Available: *www.parentech.org.* (A partnership of Ameritech and the North Central Regional Education Laboratory, the ParenTech guide will help you learn parenting tips, explore with your child and discover the world of the middle school student.)

Peck, Robert S. 1999. *Libraries, the First Amendment, and Cyberspace: What You Need to Know.* Chicago: American Library Association.

Peck, Robert S. and Ann K. Symons. "Kids Have First Amendment Rights, Too." *American Libraries* 28 (September 1997): 64–65.

"Peril and Promise: Teens by the Numbers," *Newsweek* (May 10, 1999): 38–39.

Symons, Ann K. "The Smart Web Primer, Part 2: Sizing up Sites; How to Judge What You Find on the Web." *School Library Journal* (April 1, 1997). (Also online at: *www.slj.com/articles/articles/19970401_5654.asp*).

Turow, Joseph. *The Internet and the Family: The View from Parents, the View from the Press.* 1999. Report series no. 27. Philadelphia: The Annenberg Public Policy Center of the University of Pennsylvania. (Also online at: *www.appcpenn.org*).

U.S. Department of Education, Office of Educational Research and Improvement. *Parents Guide to the Internet* [Online]. Available: *www.ed.gov/pubs/parents/internet.html* [November 1997].

Web66 [Website]. Available: *web66/coled.unm.edu/schools.html.* (Find the Websites of hundreds of elementary and secondary schools in the U.S. and worldwide.)

Wilton (Connecticut) Public Library [Website]. Available: *www. wiltonlibrary.org.*

World Almanac 2000. 1999. New York: World Almanac: 391.

Chapter 5

Steering Kids to Solo Navigation: Implementing Internet Service for Young People

Carolyn Noah

Remember the first time you held a set of car keys in your hand? Ready to take to the road, you were full of confidence, especially if you happened to be in your teenage years. You prepared for your first solo drive by practicing, understanding how to exercise good judgment, and learning about defensive driving. It wasn't your first time behind the wheel. An adult acted as coach, advised you about hazards of the road, and made sure you were ready for navigational responsibility.

The driver's ed analogy works for preparing young people to use the Internet in public libraries, too. Young people who have learned to exercise good judgment, have had plenty of practice and adult supervision, and understand their responsibilities are able Internet users. Their parents understand the benefits of the resource, and they are not interested in tearing up the highway to eliminate access to a troublesome intersection.

Effective Internet service for young people is implemented by libraries that provide thorough "drivers' training." Libraries that initiate community dialog about the value and liabilities of the Internet, prepare their staff well, and provide lots of chances for parents and children to learn together are successful. Preparation for success includes a range of components. They are:

- Ample training for youth services staff
- Thoughtful planning
- Effective policy
- Welcoming learning opportunities for families, children, and young adults

AMPLE TRAINING FOR YOUTH SERVICES STAFF

First, the staff working with young people must be able instructors. An overview to training issues can be found in "Children and the Internet: A Perfect Match," a PowerPoint presentation available online at *www.ala.org/ symons/match/* that provides an introduction to the issues and some playful Internet activities. Staff will be familiar and comfortable with the way the Internet works, through formal or informal training.

Training should include general information on the Net and its applications, from ftp and telnet to mail, chat, and the World Wide Web. Though applications become transparent as they are integrated on the Web, understanding their functions and how they operate in the Web environment is useful as staff examines the practical issues in implementing Internet programs. For example, as libraries began Internet access with few public computers, many prohibited the use of e-mail and chat. Not only do both applications have legitimate use in the learner's world, but enforcing the ban ranges from challenging to impossible.

Consider the benefits and potential liabilities. The Children's Partnership provides *The Parents' Guide to the Information Superhighway (www.childrenspartnership. org/bbar/pbpg.html)*, an excellent guide to framing the issues. The Internet can, for example, help level the playing field among learners from many environments, rural and urban; help young people with special needs get access that would not be available otherwise; and help children to become part of a world community of learners, sharing information with peers anywhere. What the Internet can't do, as the library staff knows (but parents often don't), is solve every information need or make children better learners than they already are.

Like kids, adults need to be able to distinguish Internet junk from treasure, so include information about evaluating Websites. A good starting point for evaluation is the *Librarian's Guide to Cyberspace for Parents & Kids (www.ala.org/parentspage/greatsites/selection.html)*. Though there is plenty of literature about Website evaluation, the questions staff should consider don't have to be intimidating. At the most basic level, ask the following questions.

- Who is responsible for the Website? Is the author or sponsoring organization credible?
- What is the purpose of the site? Is it apparent who the audience is?
- Is the site design easy to navigate and understand?
- Is the content accurate and age appropriate?

Knowledge of the ongoing discussion about filtering software and how it functions will be a valuable tool in the staff maintenance kit. According to ALA's *Libraries and the Internet Toolkit* (*www.ala.org/internettoolkit/index.html*), ". . . the problem with filters is they don't work very well. They block a lot of good information that many people might find useful for their jobs, school, or health needs and they don't block all the 'bad stuff.'" You can and should talk about this complicated issue in layperson's terms, but know that there is plenty of documentation, too. A 1997 undertaking called "TIFAP: The Internet Filtering Project," conducted by Karen Schneider with a large group of professional librarians, documented exactly how filters work and don't work. (The TIFAP report is available at *www.bluehighways.com/tifap/*.) Schneider noted on the electronic discussion list PUBLIB in early 2000 that she observed that neither filtering software technology nor its effectiveness had improved significantly. An excellent staff training presentation by Hershey School librarian Carrie Gardner on how filtering software works, "Public Internet Access: What About Filtering?" is available on the American Library Association's Website at *www.ala.org/symons/filtering/*.

THOUGHTFUL PLANNING

Before libraries can energize their Internet programs externally, plenty must happen within the library walls. You can start by building internal consensus about your library's procedures. Not only must they support library policy, but all of the library's staff must be willing to support them. For example, if the children's room relies upon staff from the Reference department at times, everyone should be involved in making some decisions. The following points should be among the questions considered.

- Will you require that people reserve time at the computer? Reserved time may be fair to users, but staff pay a high toll to manage the program.
- Will you post a Code of Conduct so that young people understand their privileges and responsibilities?
- Can users print from the Web? If so, will your library be able to underwrite the cost of the print cartridges and paper?
- Can you accommodate users who want to save information? Some libraries provide clean, blank disks at cost so that people can search at the library and take information home.
- Where will you place Internet terminals? Young people may require extensive help, but it's important to observe their privacy as well.

Once the staff is primed, the public aspect of bringing up effective Internet service begins. Preparation includes creating opportunities for public discussion, making sure library policies are clearly written and posted, and providing useful, exciting and easy access to great Internet resources.

By initiating public discussion about Internet service, youth services librarians can demonstrate their interest and concern to parents, teachers, and others concerned with young people in the community. Try holding an open forum or "Internet Cafe" at the library, or ask to be on the agenda at the local parent-teacher organization at your area school. Use the opportunity to show some great sites, explain your library's policy and approach, and talk about how kids can be safe on the Internet. In general, parents are anxious about the technology if they are less familiar with it than their kids. By providing a non-threatening introduction and an opportunity to ask questions, some of that anxiety can be diffused. When parents are worried about the Internet, it's important to acknowledge the legitimacy of their concerns.

It's equally important to explain clearly why young people's needs can only be addressed by the entire array of legally protected information on the Internet. While it is tempting to talk about young people's information needs in library-speak, jettison jargon when talking to parents. Save and share examples of real young people with genuine needs that have been answered by electronic resources. Profile kids who have managed sophisticated research projects by locating experts who are willing to share their insight and enthusiasm through the Internet using chat and e-mail, or identify others who have managed a long-distance move by keeping in touch with their old homes using the Internet. Acknowledge that young adults have legitimate research needs on topics like sexually transmitted diseases and gang violence that require them to use a wide range of resources. Remind parents that when their families both share expectations that young navigators will explore responsibly and spend some time engaged together in their projects, their children will be safe on the Net.

When discussing these issues with the public, remember to steer clear of library jargon. Start a translation table to remind you to convert jargon to plain English, like this:

Library Jargon	Plain English
Intellectual freedom	Free access to information
Full-text databases	Magazine and newspaper articles
URLs	Internet addresses
Critical thinking skills	Skills for evaluating information
Authority	Expertise
Boolean logic	Well-defined searches

Other preparations will help to make the service run smoothly. If your library has a Website, make sure a youth services page is developed. It should be contemporary, lively, and relevant. Just as important, it should provide links to sites and pages that your staff recommends. Include a policy statement link so that your understandings and expectations are clear.

Support your library's Website policy by providing links to information about safe navigation. "Surfing the Web Safely," an excellent compilation of Internet safety pages, can be found on ALA's Website at *www.ala.org/teach-in/ surf.html.*

Set the youth services page to be the home page on computers in the children's area of the library. If your library does not have a home page, consider using a kid-friendly search site as the home page, for example, the "Kids'

Click!" Website managed by the Ramapo-Catskill Library System (*sunsite.berkeley.edu/KidsClick!/*). Like a number of other sites, Kids' Click! includes only sites that have been selected by librarians and indexed by subject. (For those who want to see it through a librarian's eyes, there's even a link to the index page according to Dewey.) Be aware of local school assignments and compile bookmark files for young researchers. To make the Internet an indispensable service for children, export and share your bookmark files with the teachers who originate the assignments. In this sample, note that the bookmark properties have been edited to make them clearer.

Bookmarks for Ms. Ferro's 11th grade Biogenetics Project

- Access Excellence: Biotech
  www.accessexcellence.org/AB/
- Ask An Expert: Biology / Scientific American
  www.scientificamerican.com/askexpert/biology/index.html
- Basics of DNA Fingerprinting/ University of Washington class project
  www.biology.washington.edu/fingerprint/dnaintro.html
- Blazing a Genetic Trail / Howard Hughes Medical Institute
  www.hhmi.org/GeneticTrail/
- Gene Almanac / DNA Learning Center
  vector.cshl.org/
- Genetic Science Learning Center / University of Utah
  gslc.genetics.utah.edu/

- Understanding Gene Testing: an NCI Self-Learning
  Primer/National Institutes of Health
  *rex.nci.nih.gov/PATIENTS/INFO_TEACHER/
  Gene_testing/frame2. html*

EFFECTIVE POLICY

Youth services staff should be conversant with the library's
philosophical approach to the Internet, its policy, and the
practices adopted by the youth services department. Important documents that every person working with young
people should know are the American Library
Association's "Library Bill of Rights" and its interpreta-
tions, especially, "Free Access to Libraries for Minors."
The staff will understand how to find and evaluate Internet
information, as well as communicate easily about the process. Finally, and not least important, it's important to
know trends in young people's interests and some great
kid-friendly sites to recommend.

Where personal opinions and professional policies on
young people's access to the Internet collide, a challenging professional dilemma arises. Youth services and library
administration must speak coherently about the importance of Internet information for children and young
adults. Libraries that provide thoughtful training opportunities for their staff can build the high level of consensus that makes their message positive, clear and consistent.

An excellent policy example comes from the Milford
(Massachusetts) Town Library.

Milford Town Library Web Site Policy

The Milford Town Library web site is provided as an electronic service to people who are unable use our facility at the present time, or who prefer to receive some of our services via the Internet. While our web site cannot provide the full range of services that we give in our library building, we consider it a valuable tool for communication. We also hope that many people who use our site will also visit us in person in our library building. We welcome your suggestions and comments. The Milford Town Library is dedicated to providing free, easy, equal and confidential access to all forms of human expression.

The Internet offers access to a wealth of information that can be personally, professionally and culturally enriching. Library staff have attempted to identify on the Milford Town Library's web site specific starting points for searches and links to sources on the Internet which are consistent with the Library's Collection Development Policy. But, because the Internet is a vast and unregulated information network, sites on the Internet change often, rapidly and unpredictably. The Library assumes no responsibility for any damages, direct or indirect, arising from use of its electronic services or its connections to the Internet.

The Library cannot protect users from information and images that they might find offensive or disturbing. It is each user's responsibility to exercise critical judgment in evaluating the validity of information accessed via the Internet through this web site. We advise parents to monitor and supervise their children's Internet use and to talk with their own children about

Internet safety issues in relation to family values and boundaries.

(Reprinted with permission of the Milford Town Library, Milford, Massachusetts; Linda Wright, Director)

WELCOMING LEARNING OPPORTUNITIES FOR FAMILIES, CHILDREN, AND YOUNG ADULTS

To make the Internet a friendlier place, integrate welcoming learning opportunities for children and families into library programming. Here are a few success stories.

Reading Public Library: Netguide

The Reading (Massachusetts) Public Library offers parent/child Internet classes on weekend mornings. In the classes, parent-child teams learn to reach great sites from a previously selected "library," how to navigate the World Wide Web, and how to use a search engine.

Netguide programs, pioneered by Lorainne Barry, Kimberly Lynn, and Susan Beauregard at the Reading Public Library, made Internet converts of lots of families at a variety of Massachusetts libraries. In these programs, young adolescents applied and were trained to be Internet trainers for other library users. In order to participate, the youths signed contracts, participated in four classes, and committed themselves to being available. Their training included information about the Internet, a session on critical thinking skills, and opportunities to practice proficiency (upon which they were tested). The result: young people and their families who were conversant and comfortable with the Net.

READING PUBLIC LIBRARY

Netguide Contract

Please read and sign this contract after discussing the terms with a librarian.

Position Description: Netguides are students trained to use the Internet and to teach other young adults to use the Internet.

Training: The Library will provide four one hour Internet training sessions. Schedules will be arranged according to training group needs.

Students must attend all training sessions.

Students must spend at least four hours either at the Library, school or home practicing Internet skills.

Certification and Teaching: Upon successful completion of the Internet training and proficiency requirements, students will become Certified Internet Experts able to work as Netguides. Each Netguide will conduct at least two one hour young adult Internet training classes at the Library.

Internet Consultants: Interested students may apply to become Internet Consultants. Consultants will run an Internet Help Desk to assist and advise Library customers on Internet usage. Desk hours will vary according to need and student schedules.

I have read this contract and discussed it with a Librarian. I agree to fulfill these obligations.

Student Signature:_____

Librarian Signature:_____

All Netguide positions are volunteer positions.
Reading Public Library
64 Middlesex Avenue
Reading, MA 01867
781–944–0840
reading@noble.mass.edu
http://www.readingpl.org

Netguide Class Outlines

Class 1: Introduction to the Internet

    1. The Internet: background and history

    2. Information available on the Internet

    3. Information not available on the Internet

    4. Critical thinking skills

    5. Internet access at the library vs. from home or work

    6. The World Wide Web (WWW)

    7. Internet sites

    8. Internet addresses

    9. Search engines or "web navigators"

    10. Questions

Class 2: The World Wide Web

    1. The WWW: what is it?

    2. Maneuvering through the WWW

    3. Critical thinking skills revisited

    4. Internet addresses or URLs

    5. Search engines or web navigators

    6. Printing and downloading

    7. Graphical access

    8. Questions

Class 3: The Internet in Depth

    1. Telnet

    2. Gopher

    3. Bulletin Boards

    4. Newsgroups

    5. Chat

    6. E-mail

7. ISPs: Internet service providers

8. Review critical thinking skills, inputting Internet addresses, search engines, printing and downloading

9. Miscellaneous

10. Questions

Class 4: Teaching and Customer Service Tips

1. Teaching is hard.

What are some of the problems teachers have to deal with?

1.

2.

3.

4.

5.

What is the most important quality in a teacher?

1.

2. Teach us

Volunteers may select a slip of paper with a task written on it. After a minute of reflection the volunteer must teach the group how to perform the task.

3. Encouragement

Words of encouragement are very important to students of any age. What are some good ones?

1.

2.

3.

4.

4. Ask me

Acknowledge and answer questions throughout the session. If you don't know an answer, admit it and try to find out the answer.

(Reprinted with permission of the Reading Public Library, Reading, Massachusetts.)

Marlborough Public Library: Safe and Healthy on the Internet

Safe and Healthy on the Internet was a program conducted for teens and parents at the Marlborough (Massachusetts) Public Library, by young adult librarian Susan Alatalo. Following a community scare about Internet predators, her goal was to open a dialog with families about the value of the Internet and ways kids can be safe on it. She began with a discussion among school and public library staff and the police department, who moved from polarized opinions about access to an agreement to seek ways to present the whole Internet picture. Having built consensus among the child advocacy group, the library promoted a panel featuring a variety of points of view and lots of questions and answers. The program helped to diffuse community panic and provide some realistic grounding for young people about safe navigation. It enlisted the police department in seeing access as a multi-dimensional issue.

"The young adults who participated have a better sense of the role of the library in providing Internet access and a much clearer idea of their own responsibilities," Susan asserted. "Another outcome has been to encourage kids to be more communicative about their Internet experiences, narrowing the opportunity for dangerous situations."

As concern about young adult safety has gained momentum, the Marlborough community has taken a comprehensive approach to protecting young adults from violence of all kinds. Through the work of a violence protection task force (dealing with the Internet as well as other issues) on which many concerned adults participate, students have the chance to communicate with other young people about issues concerning them, to participate in events planned by multiple agencies, and are encouraged to seek positive solutions to their problems.

Free and open access to all electronic resources flourishes in public libraries when youth services staff are well-prepared, public dialog has been encouraged, and ample opportunities for families to explore the Internet in a constructive environment are provided. Despite all preparations, some communities may not be prepared to accept complete access. In these cases, a compromise must be sought.

Joshua's Hyde N' Seek Page

At the Joshua Hyde Library, the Sturbridge, Massachusetts public library, trustees grappled with complaints from a vocal minority of the community who asserted that unfiltered access to the Internet was dangerous to children. Library director Ellie Chesebrough investigated, and learned that the single Internet access terminal (which was the room's sole access to CD-ROMs as well) in the children's room had been used by three children during the survey month, and two had been accompanied by parents. Nonetheless, the library board of trustees listened seriously to the complaint. While reaffirming their commitment to free access to information and discussing the issues publicly, the board proposed a satisfactory compromise. Computers in the main portion of the library remain unfiltered. In the children's room, filtering options on easy-to-use search engines have been switched on. In addition to the library's "Policy for Public Use of the Internet," the trustees, led by member Jim Douglas, drafted an information page for parents which is posted on the library's home page and at the children's room computer. It states:

About the Selected Resources on "Joshua's Hyde N' Seek" Page and Filters

The Subject Directories and Search Engines recommended on Joshua's Hyde N' Seek page were selected on the basis of their appropriateness for children, age 5–12, in terms of ease of use, as well as the content, coverage, and currency of their databases.

The suggested search engines employ various filters that are either "built-in" or include a feature that allows the user to employ a filter as an option. For example, Ask Jeeves for Kids first searches a database of selected sites and then conducts a parallel search filtered through SurfWatch; Searchopolis uses the Bess database to eliminate adult and other objectionable material. If you would like to conduct a non-filtered search, please ask the librarian for assistance.

Note: Filters can reduce, but not totally eliminate, material that users may find offensive or objectionable and may, at the same time, block access to legitimate and useful resources.

(Reprinted with permission of the Joshua Hyde Public Library, Sturbridge, Massachusetts.)

In conclusion, no one's first solo drive is perfect. However, Internet service for young people cruises smoothly onto the information highway when staff is trained to instruct young users on navigating the Web, when plenty of planning goes into passing the driver's test, when policies or rules of the road are clear, and when children and families have the opportunity to learn in a positive, safe environment.

RESOURCES

Access Excellence. 2000. *About Biotech* [Online]. Available: *www.accessexcellence.org* /AB/. [February 4, 2000].

American Library Association. 1999. *Librarian's Guide to Cyberspace for Parents and Kids: Selection* [Online]. Available: *www.ala.org/parentspage/greatsites/selection. html.*

American Library Association. 2000. *Libraries and the Internet Toolkit: Tips and Guidance for Managing and Communicating About the Internet* [Online]. Available: *www.ala.org/internettoolkit/index.html.*

American Library Association. 1980. *The Library Bill of Rights* [Online]. Available: *www.ala.org/work/freedom/ lbr.html.*

American Library Association. 1999. *Surfing the Web Safely* [Online]. Available: *www.ala.org/teach-in/surf. html.*

Children's Parnership. 1998. *The Parent's Guide to the Information Superhighway* [Online]. Available: *www. childrenspartnership.org/pub/pbpg1.html.*

DNA Learning Center, Cold Springs Harbor Laboratory. *Gene Almanac* [Online]. Available: *vector.cshl.org/.* [Undated].

Gardner, Carrie. American Library Association. 1998. *Public Internet Access: What About Filtering?* [Online]. Available: *www.ala.org/symons/filtering/.*

Howard Hughes Medical Institute. 1999. *Blazing a Genetic Trail* [Online]. Available: *www.hhmi.org/Genetic Trail/.*

National Institutes of Health. 1996. *Understanding Gene Testing: an NCI Self-Learning Primer* [Online]. Available: *rex.nci.nih.gov/PATIENTS/INFO_TEACHER/ Gene_testing/frame2.html*.

Noah, Carolyn. 1998. *American Library Association Children and the Internet: A Perfect Match* [Online]. Available: *www.ala.org/symons/match/*.

Schneider, Karen. "Filtering Update" [PUBLIB list posting] Available: *sunsite.berkeley.edu/PubLib/archive/0002/ 0303.html*. [February 18, 2000].

Schneider, Karen. 1998. *The Internet Filtering Project* [Online]. Available: *www.bluehighways.com/tifap*.

Scientific American. 2000. "Ask The Experts: Biology" [Online]. Available: *www.scientificamerican.com/ askexpert/biology/index.html*.

University of Utah. 2000. *Genetic Science Learning Center* [Online]. Available: *gslc.genetics.utah.edu/*.

University of Washington. 1994. *Class Project: Basics of DNA Fingerprinting* [Online]. Available: *www.biology. washington.edu/fingerprint/dnaintro.html*.

Chapter 6

Working with Trustees

Gordon M. Conable

CONTEXT

The Internet offers unprecedented challenges for library policy makers. The technology is transforming libraries at a terrific pace, and the transformation has major implications for the institution, touching on all aspects of operations, funding, facilities, staffing, operations, and public perception. While the core mission of the public library remains unchanged, its means of fulfilling that mission are being expanded and altered to such an extent that the survival of the institution may be at risk.

Until the last five years of the twentieth century, the public library was a solidly print-based, custodial institution designed around the technology of the book. The library acquired, organized, stored, and circulated information in physical formats among its community of users. The

Internet frees the library from its dependence upon locally acquired collections as its primary means of meeting the information needs of its users; but at the same time, it threatens the continued existence of a book-based institution. The implications of the technology cannot be underestimated.

New technologies have spelled the end of occupations and institutions in the past. Perhaps few institutions have been displaced as quickly and completely as the livery stable was by the automobile, for example. But today, the revolution in information technology clearly suggests that the traditional print-centered custodial model of the library is over. At least this is a perception that is taking root among both members of the public and some elected officials. Lest this sound alarmist, it should be noted that the technology also offers a great opportunity to revitalize the library in undreamed of ways and to solidly reposition it as an essential public service for years to come. For libraries, technology has produced effects some of which are transitory, some transformational, and some which have reinforced the importance of the institution's role in society.

A healthy economy—hopefully not transitory—has resulted in a renaissance of library construction in much of the country, and in many communities the future of the library has never looked brighter. But there are critics who ponder the wisdom of constructing buildings for an institution that may be obsolete. For example, in opposition to a March 2000 California ballot proposal for state bonds to finance $350 million in library construction, state senator Ray Haynes wrote: "With new computer technology and the growth of the Internet, the library improvements funded by this bond may be obsolete in five years . . . Information can be retrieved and exchanged much more conveniently—and at a much lower cost—through the Internet. This bond is actually more expensive than offering FREE Internet service to every school child in California!" (*California Voter Information Guide, March 7, 2000 Primary Election*, 19.) Public library funding which declined sharply in much of the country at the end of the 1980s and in the early 1990s is rebounding in many areas even as traditional library use—measured in the circulation of books—may be flat or declining.

Libraries with Internet connections, on the other hand, are seeing surging demand and lines of people waiting for available machines. The Internet brings unprecedented quantities and types of information into the library. Since the individual at the computer determines both the information sought and its mode of retrieval, the Internet bypasses the staff mediation represented by professional collection development. The library no longer exerts the same control over the content it provides that it did traditionally, and that changes everything. There has always been a tension in librarianship between a commitment to give the people what they want and to give the people what librarians think they ought to want. Given the choice, most people would rather do it themselves.

The library profession has a strong record of defending the rights of library users and librarians are recognized as advocates and defenders of free expression. With the Internet, this role is more important than ever. The ideal of the library as the embodiment of the marketplace of ideas has a long tradition, but the content of that marketplace has always been a little threatening. Putting the

Internet in the library provides an opportunity for communities to confront and discover anew the reality of the range of speech that flourishes in the world. Librarians have provided crucial leadership in litigation that has resulted in Supreme Court decisions which establish First Amendment rights in cyberspace that equal or exceed those in print or in broadcast media. Americans enjoy a freedom of expression that encompasses much more than that which has been represented on the shelves of most public libraries. The dissonance between that reality and the image of the public library as it still exists in many people's minds can be truly breathtaking.

Librarians and policy makers are faced with the necessity of confronting these changes and thinking about them productively. But the sailors on a ship in stormy seas riding out a storm are rarely in a position to redesign their vessel or rethink the nature of oceanic travel.

WHO'S IN CHARGE HERE?

The vast majority of American public libraries are a function of local government, although the laws that establish them demonstrate an almost dizzying variety of governance structures. In general, the unit of government that provides the major funding for the service sets library policies. Most public libraries have boards of trustees—appointed or elected officials who serve either as policy-making and governing bodies for libraries or who sit in an advisory capacity to municipal governments or other jurisdictions where elected officials retain policy and budgetary control of the library.

Boards

Library boards are usually composed of laypersons with a strong commitment to library service and with significant standing in their community. Most often these are volunteers who are uncompensated or only minimally compensated for their service. The time they spend on their duties as board members is generally limited to one or two board meetings a month, the preparatory time necessary for these meetings, some additional committee work, and representation of the library at other meetings and in public. Of course, trustee involvement in library fundraising, building projects, advocacy, and volunteer efforts can greatly increase this time commitment. Significant controversy arising out of any aspect of library policy or operations can also greatly impact the demands placed upon trustees.

Staff

Library directors and librarians who staff public libraries do not set library policy, although they implement the policies established by their governing bodies. They also advise policy-makers in drafting and adopting policy that the staff is then charged with implementing. The distinction between policy and procedure, though often a little muddy in practice, is critical to understanding who has responsibility for a library's policies and their consequences. But in public libraries, even more than in many other local government services, the close and longstanding relationship between the board and the library director and her staff increases the opportunity for the policy makers to realistically address the operational reality of the policies they set.

NEW TECHNOLOGY, DIFFERENT RULES?

Most library policies have evolved in response to the operational requirements of acquiring, organizing, storing, lending, and retrieving information in physical storage units—books and other formats, including sound recordings, periodicals, and videotapes. In the best circumstances, these policies are designed to facilitate individual use of publicly owned resources in a manner that protects the materials and reflects the underlying function of the institution. To the extent that a library's policies reflect the core values of librarianship—a commitment to First Amendment values and the preservation, dissemination and retrieval of recorded human expression—they may operate independently of format. Thus many policies may be broadly applicable to library operations regardless of the manner—or technology—by which information is provided to the library user.

It is useful to approach Internet-related policy issues from this framework, since it helps clarify questions that might be obscured merely by the fact that the technology has changed. Basically, the library user is still retrieving information through the library's resources and services.

A recent example illustrates this point. When libraries started buying and circulating videotapes in the 1980s, some of them structured this service as if the fact that the medium was different suggested that it should be treated differently. That is, some libraries, in contrast with a long-established tradition of lending books without charge, started levying a rental fee for videotapes. Open access policies, which allowed all users to borrow any material that they had a constitutional right to read or view, were sometimes changed to set an age limit for the use of videotapes. The rationale for these changes—the cost of the material, for example—was generally inconsistent if accurate comparisons were made to the library's policies covering books of equal or greater value. It is far more likely that the distinctions being made were really based upon uneasiness about content and the visual nature of the medium, concerns that may also apply to consideration of the Internet.

From a functional viewpoint, however, neither the technology nor the format should make any difference in the way libraries view their purpose or their mission. Unless they are completely superseded by a superior, cheaper nongovernmental means of distributing information, public libraries will remain the guardians of a great public good: the provision of information to all, regardless of economic means, as a method of insuring the well-being of an informed, self-governing populace.

WHAT TRUSTEES NEED TO KNOW

In order to carefully address policy issues surrounding the Internet, trustees need to stay informed in a number of changing areas. These include the legal context in which they operate, the nature of the technology, and the expectations of the public(s) they serve.

First, as boards examine their legal context, it is surprising that many people—including some trustees—may not understand that public libraries are government agencies. To some degree this is because libraries have a long tradition of heavy volunteer involvement and because of the traditional image of the library and the librarian in many communities. But government agencies they are, supported by taxes, and as such they operate under a framework of laws from the U.S. Constitution through local ordinance that dictate and limit the policy options available to their trustees. This is why all policies adopted by a board must be in compliance with local, state, and federal law, including the First Amendment. It is therefore essential that trustees have access to competent legal counsel when they consider and adopt policy.

Failing to seek and heed legal advice may result in extended litigation and adverse impacts on the institution, as the Loudoun County, Virginia Library Board found when it was sued (and lost) over a policy that imposed flawed Internet filtering software on all the library's Internet computers.

In practice, few libraries are ever sued over policy. However, awareness of the current state of legislation and litigation concerning Internet access and filtering, provided by your attorney, is likely to temper rash moves into policy decisions that could seriously backfire. The American Library Association's Office for Intellectual Freedom maintains a Website with a current appraisal of the state of the law concerning Internet policies, including a series of legal memos from a law firm specializing in First Amendment litigation before the Supreme Court. While the material posted there is no substitute for legal advice from a board's attorney, it provides a good starting point for trustees considering the likely ramifications of the various approaches to Internet policy questions most likely to be brought before them.

Second, trustees ought to be familiar with the nature of

the technology as competent Internet users themselves. This may seem to be a daunting requirement for some who joined the board out of a love for books and who may still be dubious about the place of computers in libraries. However, too often library policy has been approached in a reactive manner by trustees whose personal knowledge and experience of the Net is limited to what they've read in the paper, heard on the radio, seen on TV, or been told by constituents. Several years ago a library director at a large urban library in the Southwest arranged an Internet training session for her board, most of who had little experience with computers. After two hours of showing them how to use a browser to access subject matter of interest to each of them, she stopped the session and asked them how they felt about all the pornography. None of them had encountered any at all, and the point was made that the Net is not actually an unstoppable river of smut arriving spontaneously on the screen of any computer which happens to be hooked up to a network.

Today, our trustees also need a better understanding of the nature of the technology than public discourse about filtering software has yet provided. Concerns about sexual content, hate speech, and other material on the Internet have made filtering software seem desirable, necessary, or even inevitable to some elected officials and members of the public. However, all filtering software is seriously flawed, both in what it purports to do and what it actually delivers. The speed of growth and change on the Internet makes any human review of the content of *all* Web pages a clear impossibility. Computer-assisted (or conducted) review of Web content remains—and will probably forever remain—flawed at best. Trustees need information about how the software works and its limitations lest marketing claims appear credible. Despite all marketing claims to the contrary, tests of existing software invariably demonstrate both overbroad blocking and underblocking of whatever it is that the software attempts to prevent access to. That is, harmless (or useful) information will be blocked, and offensive or even illegal material will get through.

For a public institution, blocking information that is protected speech in an attempt to prevent access to information that is illegal raises serious constitutional issues. Congress and legislatures keep trying to pass legislation requiring public libraries to install filters which will block legally obscene speech and child pornography, but those are legal standards which are adjudicated in court and not the opinion of software programs, software manufacturers, or librarians. There *is* no software that would comply with these proposed laws without also blocking a great deal of speech that is legal and protected under the law. Therefore, the proposed laws are likely to be litigated and to be eventually declared unconstitutional, as earlier attempts have been. The fact that senators and members of Congress who should know better continue to cynically offer these proposals is no justification for library trustees and other local officials to join them in setting local policy.

Requiring adults to access the Internet through blocking software is almost certainly unconstitutional. Requiring minors to access the Internet through filters that block speech that is constitutionally protected for them—most of the speech that current filters block—is also constitutionally suspect. On the other hand, offering users a choice to limit their Internet access through personal use of self-imposed filtering software—either through a menu choice or by use of a filtered workstation when unfiltered workstations are also available—would probably survive constitutional challenge. Whether that also equates to good library service is an ethical question.

Public expectations of libraries were shaped in a pre-Internet era. They frequently include an unstated assumption that the contents of the library have been vetted for acceptability and that some types of material cannot be found through the library's services. In an age of computers, this assumption is obsolete. In most jurisdictions, policy responses to Internet access are still a work in process. While most public libraries offer unfiltered Internet access, a few (less than 20 percent) offer a filtered option. Some filter all computers in children's areas. Some libraries limit children to the use of filtered computers under any circumstance. This approach is constitutionally dubious, at least for older children. Others have some filtered computers but allow children to use any computer. Still others leave it to the parent to direct which machine a child uses. Some libraries participate in enforcing the parent's wishes to limit their children to filtered machines in some manner; other libraries decline to do so. Generally, the more responsibility a library takes for what the user can or cannot access, the knottier the legal issues are likely to be. On the other hand, failing to acknowledge political realities surrounding this may leave the library vulnerable to media attention, political pressure, patron anxiety, or other unwanted attention. At times it may seem like a no-win situation.

WHERE THE RUBBER HITS THE ROAD

Because the technology, the law, and the territory are constantly changing, a certain wariness of easy answers is probably healthy. Boards (and librarians) have a public trust to maintain. They must be open to public input, comment, and criticism. They should be willing to take principled stands. They should be committed to preserving the values of the institution and the institution itself.

This means that trustees need the information necessary not only to make informed policy decisions, but also to be able to articulate the reasons for them and defend them against challenges and potential criticism. Citing the First Amendment is rarely particularly effective in the face of a vocal citizen who believes that the Internet should be filtered and has no concept of how difficult it would be to design and implement a defensible technology approach to regulating Internet content. The fact that filters are widely used in public schools—where their use may compromise not only the educational function of the institution but also the rights of students and faculty—does not help the discussion. The "safety" of children is an argument difficult to answer in any context, whether or not actual harm can be demonstrated. Obscenity laws on the books are rarely utilized, but that fact does not prevent legislators from imposing ever more dubious limitation on legal speech in an attempt to stamp out sexual information of all sorts. In the face of these home truths, library boards who stand for free Internet access may find themselves under pressure from friends, family members, and others whom they respect, just as when these same library boards have stood up against demands that books be censored. The courage that is required is no less because the technology has changed; the clarity and vision which is called for is no less, but neither is the threat to freedom if they succumb to the pressures of the moment.

As with all technological revolutions, over time people will continue to improve their understanding of the advantages the Internet brings and how to live with its downside. It is worth considering that, when all is said and done, the concerns about content on the Internet are likely to have a much smaller impact on the library as an institution than the fact that the Internet exists at all. While the Web has yet to replace print and print-based institutions—publishing, libraries, and bookstores—it is transforming all of them, and it may yet supplant them. In the meantime, those three institutions must adapt to the new technology and attempt to integrate it functionally if they are to survive even a little longer.

Chapter 7

Say the Right Thing!
Twelve Rules for Answering
Tough Questions

Patricia Glass Schuman

Someone once asked Woodrow Wilson how long it would take him to prepare for a ten-minute presentation. Wilson's answer: "Two weeks." What about an hour-long presentation? "One week." A two-hour speech? "I'm ready right now," he boasted.

Like Wilson, most of us could talk at length about our work and our professional opinions. But if asked to distill those thoughts down to a few measured words, we would need time for careful consideration. That's especially true when answering tough questions about the Internet and its use at your library, whether the questions are asked by a user or the media.

Many people hesitate to reach out to reporters because

they are afraid of tough or hostile questions. It may help to remember that, for the most part, the media are our friends—particularly when it comes to First Amendment and freedom of information issues.

That doesn't mean, however, that they automatically understand everything we say. Besides knowing the facts, being an effective library spokesperson means delivering your message in terms your listener can relate to and understand. And you need to repeat your message. Your goal as library spokesperson is not to be viewed as smart and erudite or to inundate your listener with facts. Your goal is to communicate effectively and win support for your position.

With practice, anyone can anticipate tough or probing questions, step into the spotlight, and be a confident spokesperson. It takes time and effort, but it will save you anxiety in the end. As someone who benefited from receiving media training when I was President-elect of the American Library Association, and who has survived almost 100 media interviews since then, I can assure you that most experienced spokespeople make it through tough times by learning to turn anxiety into opportunity.

You can do it by following a few simple communications rules. They will help you when speaking to reporters, board members, the Kiwanis, an angry customer, or even your mother.

MEDIA DO'S AND DON'TS

Rule 1

Don't be afraid to ask your own questions. Who is your questioner? If it is the media, what is the name and type of publication or station? Find out the reporter's topic, angle, and deadline. If you do not feel qualified to address the issue or if you are uncomfortable with the angle, say so. Suggest other angles or sources of information.

Rule 2

Be prepared to answer the standard who, what, when, where, why, and how questions. Have supporting facts and examples available, or know where you can get them. But don't use them all at once!

Rule 3

Be positive, honest, and straightforward. Offer facts, not conjecture, and be sure to get your positive statement up front. Tell the truth, be clear about whom you are speaking for, whether it is yourself, your library, or library association. If you don't know an answer, tell your interviewer that you will get back to them or direct them to the appropriate person. Never assume that anything you say is "off the record." It can, and probably will, be used. And never say, "No comment." If you are asked for information you can't release, tell the reporter that you can't release the information and explain why.

Rule 4

Pause before you answer a question. Listen—really listen—to the questioner. Suspend all judgment of the individual and identify the issue. Take the time to think about what you want to say and the best way to say it.

Try to empathize with the questioner. What is he or she really asking and why? By actively listening, you're showing you've given the question serious consideration. If a question has an obvious bias, try to use positive language. For example: "You evidently have strong feelings about this," or "I respect your views, but let me give you another perspective."

Rule 5

When necessary, reframe the question. A reporter asks, "Why does your library encourage kids to look at pornography by letting them use the Internet?" Don't respond negatively. Strip away loaded words by saying, "Let me be sure I understand the question: It's about how children are using the Internet in our library."

Rule 6

Beware of manipulation. Some reporters may ask leading questions. They often start by stating an idea and asking you to agree or to disagree with it. For example, a reporter might say, "Pat, would you agree that libraries are not doing enough to filter out pornography?" If a reporter uses this tactic, don't be pressured into a quick response. Remember Rule 4: Pause and think first. Then, make your own statement. If you don't know an answer or need more time, tell the reporter you will get back to him or her.

Rule 7

Never repeat a negative. Frame your answer in positive terms. Question: "Why do librarians encourage children to look at smut by letting them use the Internet?"

The wrong answer to that question is: "Librarians don't encourage children to look at smut." The right answer is: "Librarians care deeply about children. Our role is to guide and assist them in selecting the best materials for their needs, whether it's a good book or a good Website. We are expert Internet navigators, and we are willing and eager to help parents teach their children to use the Internet appropriately to locate quality sites."

Rule 8

Don't give one-word answers. Use every opportunity to make your point and reinforce your message. Question: "Isn't it true that librarians spend money on Internet access that could be better spent on books?"

Wrong answer: "No."

Right answer: "We believe people need information in all forms. Internet access is one more valuable learning tool, and it can sometimes provide information in a way that a single collection of books in any one library cannot."

Rule 9

Talk in soundbites. These brief, "quotable" statements

should contain an emotional response or a declaration that puts an issue into perspective. Ideally it should create a "word picture" that will make a lasting impression.

Here are some examples for questions about children and online pornography:

- "The best way to ensure your child's safety online is to be there."
- "You would not expect your child to learn to ride a bike without your help."
- "Putting blinders on children is not the answer."
- "Having the government or libraries censor is not the answer. Rather, all of us must teach children the same kind of safety measures for the Internet that we do for the mall."

Rule 10

Remember to "bridge," "flag," and "hook." These three techniques will help you take control in a variety of interview situations.

Bridging allows you to take a question and create an opportunity to make the point you want to make. There are two good bridging techniques you can use to take control of media situations.

One technique is useful if a reporter asks you a great, positive question, perhaps one of the three questions you would most like to answer. "Isn't it true that libraries are one of the few places that teach parents and children to use the Internet?"

First answer the question. Then, before the reporter asks the next question, state another one you would like to answer. "While we're talking about the role of librarians in teaching our users about the Internet, let me share with you a question I'm often asked: 'With the vast amount of information available on the Internet, how can parents possibly know exactly what is appropriate and reliable for their child?'

"Let me answer by saying that no one parent or librarian can possibly know that. The Internet is too vast. That is why our library has developed a special children's home page to help them find appropriate Websites they'll enjoy."

The second way to use a bridge is when you are asked a question you don't want to answer: "Isn't it true that part of the problem is that librarians are unwilling to filter the Internet?" The negative question deserves a short answer, followed by a new question and longer answer. "It is true that filters are a faulty technology in a library situation. The more important question is: What are we librarians doing to help parents and their children use the Internet effectively and safely? Let me answer that (and go on to describe classes, special services, programs, and resources that the library offers)."

Flagging is a technique you can use to focus your listener's attention by putting a "flag" on the statement. This is particularly helpful with reporters who don't seem to be getting your point or in lengthy interviews where your message might get lost. For example: "The most important point I have to make is . . ." or "Here are three things you need to know . . ."

Hooking is a verbal technique that lets you trap the questioner into hearing your three important points. Example: "Mark, there are really three ways to answer your question. The first is . . ."

Rule 11

Be repetitive and "plagiarize" when necessary. Research shows that people need to hear something seven times in order to remember it. Seven may seem like a high number, but even reporters need to hear things more than once. Repeat as much as you can, work your message into your answers, and remember that neither your message nor your answer needs to be original. What you need is to be clear, concise, and likable. Share your positive and negative experiences with others. Use the *ALA Internet Toolkit*, and adapt it for your own needs.

Rule 12

Anticipate and practice. You can anticipate most hard questions and learn to answer them by practicing. Answer the worst questions you can imagine. Role-play with colleagues or, even better, non-library friends. The worst trap you can fall into is using library jargon with laypeople!

The most important thing to remember is that if you are prepared, you can be in control. If you know what to expect, you can make your key points in a persuasive, nondefensive, and interesting way.

Woodrow Wilson was right. It takes a lot of time and effort to be brief. But when you prepare yourself to talk about tough issues, you've become an effective advocate for—and an asset to—both your library and your community. Speak up, and never forget to let your passion and commitment show. You have an important story to tell!

This chapter was adapted from an article (Patricia Glass Schuman, "Say the Right Thing: Winning Strategies for Talking to the Press") originally published in School Library Journal, *September 1998, 110–111.*

Chapter 8

Talking Internet
with Elected Officials

Mark L. Smith

State and federal lawmakers have demonstrated an irrepressible urge to buy Internet connections and content for users of all types of libraries. This fortunate tendency is completely understandable and predictable. Internet in libraries represents the confluence of three time-tested, slam-dunk vote-getters: libraries, universal access, and high technology. The push to ensure that the public enjoys universal access to the Internet has caused an unprecedented level of federal and state funds to flow to libraries in the last five years. More funding is yet to come if library advocates continue to create the right message. However, recent controversies regarding sexually explicit content on the Internet should be a warning that this cornucopia of Internet related wealth—and other library funding as well—could dry up overnight if we do not remain watchful of the pitfalls inherent in the medium. Library lobbyists can also encounter other pitfalls, including misstating or overestimating the benefits of connectivity, failing to exercise foresight for the medium, and ignoring the topic when pitching more traditional library services.

This chapter is intended to alert library advocates to some of the hidden benefits and dangers of talking to elected officials, especially legislators, about the Internet.

HOW FAR WE'VE COME

In just over five years, libraries have gone from very scant to nearly universal connection to the Internet. Academic library connectivity is nearly 100 percent, public library connectivity is between 73 and 79 percent, depending on which account you read. The number of school libraries that are connected continues to grow thanks to the E-rate and other state-based initiatives. This rush to connect libraries began in the mid-1990s with such states as North Carolina, Colorado, Florida, and Hawaii taking the lead. State-based programs such as the Telecommunications Infrastructure Fund in Texas (1995), and the federal E-rate provided in the Federal Telecommunications Act of 1996, have ensured that most libraries have access to discounted infrastructure costs, ongoing connectivity charges, or both. Many states pioneered more limited programs to purchase infrastructure costs in libraries, such as California's InfoPeople project and New York's Project GAIN.

Some states have also begun content delivery via library-based Internet service, though support for content has lagged far behind support for connectivity. North Carolina was one of the first states to recognize the potential of this new high-speed data delivery network and began as early as 1994 to deploy the network to schools, libraries, and government agencies for use in information delivery and distance learning. Beginning in 1993, academic librarians and other library advocates in Texas began to envision a network—which has come to be known as TexShare—that would provide a platform for statewide library resource sharing for higher education. The concept of TexShare was adapted in Georgia's GALILEO project and, with funding from lottery sources, greatly expanded to permit access by public and school libraries as well. Both TexShare and GALILEO offer members access to shared, full-text databases. Recently, New York State introduced EmpireLink, a three-year project to provide database access through their local libraries.

What did these and other successful projects share as a common starting point? All had effective lobbyists. In some cases these were paid lobbyists, but more often they have been librarians and lay library supporters such as library users, library board members, and others who share a love of libraries. These library advocates know (and some have learned the hard way) how to talk effectively to elected officials about the Internet.

WHAT'S NEXT?

So what's the problem? Given the success of the library community in lobbying for Internet access, why should we be concerned about fashioning a careful message for legislators? While it is true that we have had unprecedented success in securing state and federal funding for library access to the Internet, this success was partly because we had articulate advocates and partly because we were in the right place at the right time.

The next round will be harder. Now that the physical network is in place, library advocates face a number of challenges as they continue their push for legislative support. Those challenges include:

- Delivering on the promise that public Internet access will provide citizens and students vast new levels of information
- Finding resources to pay for access to full-text and bibliographic information that is commercially available
- Answering concerns about the presence of sexually explicit materials and other controversial content on the Web
- Meeting the public's demand for bandwidth to receive such high-demand content as music, video, and graphics
- Re-examining how libraries can compete in a digital environment that offers the public many other alternatives that meet their information needs

Each of these points carries its own set of problems and requires its own set of arguments. Collectively, these issues force library advocates to stay aware of all the ethical, philosophical, and technical challenges that the Internet has ushered into our libraries.

We must formulate our arguments because funding access to the network is only the first step toward meeting the need. Now that the network is in place, libraries must deliver content and services via the Internet. Legislators have proven to have a sharp appetite for funding one-time hardware costs, but less interest in funding ongoing costs such as telecommunications costs and content delivery.

Chances are, as librarians approach the legislative process, they will likely be talking to their elected officials about highly defined issues such as the funding of a specific project. Or they may be speaking for or against a piece of legislation that will create a law that will govern the Internet in libraries. Even in the best of situations, citizens approaching legislators do well to think through the dynamics of not only the issue at hand, but others that may be on the legislator's mind.

WHAT MOTIVATES ELECTED OFFICIALS?

Before you can understand how to fashion your Internet message, it is instructive to spend a moment putting yourself in the position of the legislators to whom you will appeal for support. Elected officials are ordinary individuals who are in an extraordinary position—they must represent their constituencies in the process of making and enforcing laws. This situation places them under particular pressures that motivate their actions in predictable ways.

What are those predictable motivations?

- *The desire to make an impact.* Cynicism aside, elected officials put up with a lot of unglamorous work—from endless public appearances to boring committee hearings to lots of baby-kissing and glad-handing. The only reason anyone would do it is because they believe that they can make a difference and that their actions have a lasting improvement on lives. Projects with the greatest demonstrable impact carry the greatest bragging rights and, therefore, will be of the greatest appeal.

- *The tendency to want to get reelected.* Getting reelected means pleasing no less than a simple majority while simultaneously alienating no more than 49 percent. Of course, not all politicians will run for reelection, but if they are not, then a compensating drive comes into play—concern over their legacy.

- *Controversy avoidance.* The first question an elected official will likely ask about an issue is, "Who opposes this idea?" Assessing the opposition is a key element in deciding whether to take on an issue and the tolerance for opposition is surprisingly low. If a single association, small group of individuals, or even a single influential constituent has a reason to oppose an initiative, it can be very hard to find an elected official to buy into supporting the idea. Controversial ideas extend to those that are extremely costly or that require the addition of staff to government agencies. Legislative staff are trained to research this information before advising their boss on whether to support an issue.

- *Coalition building.* The flip side of controversy-avoidance is the question, "Who supports this?" If a politician believes backing an issue will solidify support among a group or groups that he or she is courting, pitching the issue will be that much easier. Coalitions extend to trading favors with other colleagues in public office.

- *Power accumulation.* It's all about power, an elusive commodity at best. Power is a combination of the size of the groups that support the official and the level of credibility and respect that official has developed among colleagues over the years. Power means nothing more than having the clout to accomplish one's goals.

- *Ideological considerations.* Everyone knows that elected officials define themselves according to ideological boundaries, especially on some so-called hot-button issues. However, this is a more complex arrangement than one might assume. Cynics will say that politicians sway in the wind of expediency, while the more generous view is that elected officials with integrity make decisions that are for the good of the majority of the people they serve. Whatever the motivation, seasoned political watchers will tell you that even though you cannot ignore party and interest affiliations, second-guessing an elected official along ideological lines can often be an error-prone strategy.

BUILDING YOUR STRATEGY

These considerations can help library advocates develop their approach and their message. Library advocates too often rely on the inherent good of their idea to sell itself. Or, if under attack, they may rely on inherent values such as First Amendment rights to defend their position. Doing so can create blinders that prevent us from seeing the issue as the legislator might. To make an Internet proposal a reality—or to prevent unwanted tampering with library

programs—we must put our ideas to a series of questions
that derive from the considerations mentioned above.

Those questions would be as follows:

- *How many people will be affected by this plan?* The
  Internet has the potential to reach great numbers of
  users through our libraries. And libraries have the potential to maximize public access to these services to
  a point approaching universal access. Can you demonstrate that your Internet-based service enhancement
  will extend either connectivity or content delivery to
  significant populations?
- *Does your idea appeal to other groups?* What other
  groups can you bring to the table when you pitch your
  idea? Information access through electronic networks
  has typically been an idea popular with many groups
  including education associations, higher education organizations, chambers of commerce, associations of
  local government officials, and community development advocates, to name a few. Time spent cultivat-
  ing these groups can be very useful.
- *Who might oppose your idea?* Chances are there are
  not many groups or individuals who will oppose
  schemes to improve library Internet connectivity and
  content delivery. However, there may be opposition
  and it may come from groups that you did not even
  know existed. In considering this question, think about
  for-profit groups that may oppose free access. Think
  also about groups that have concerns about the content of the Internet, especially those who are fearful
  about the availability of sexually explicit materials.
- *How much will it cost and what is the nature of those*

costs? These will be prime concerns for any elected official. Money is tight all around and no one wants to be accused of spending public money freely. Thus, ideas that have the greatest payoff for the least cost will fare best. But there are costs and then there are costs. Even if your idea has a price tag attached, it is best if the costs are one-time non-recurring costs. This is why it has been easier to fund connectivity projects rather than content-delivery projects.

- *What is the demonstrated payoff of this project?* Put another way, this question says, what bragging rights will the legislator who adopts your idea have when it is done, and how quickly will they arrive? The further away the event horizon, the harder it will be to gain buy-in.

- *How does this project benefit key constituent and support groups?* Before carrying a bill or supporting an idea, the legislator will want to know how it will specifically impact his or her core constituent groups. This means doing some research in the legislator's district. What colleges and universities are there? What schools would be affected? How many students will be affected? How many libraries are there in the district? How did the legislator fare with teacher groups in the last election? How about community development groups?

- *What other support does the idea have among members of the target legislator's own party and others?* Remembering that coalitions and power accumulation means gaining and keeping the cooperation and approval of other elected officials, you will want to work your proposal broadly and develop support from as many individuals in public office in both the legislative and executive branches as you can. Legislators will want to know how others view the idea, starting with influential members of the same party, other members of their party, and then influential members of the other party. One of the inherent strengths of library issues is that they tend to enjoy non-partisan support.

DEVELOPING THE RIGHT MESSAGE

In developing their message about Internet-based services in libraries, library advocates have learned the hard way that some approaches are more effective than others. Some common mistakes can trap the unsuspecting grassroots lobbyist—or even seasoned veteran—into making promises that cannot be fulfilled, or that provoke tough questions for which no answers are readily available.

Consider the following strategies when you are addressing Internet issues with legislators and other elected officials:

- *Keep it simple.* It is easy to get bogged down in technical details of connectivity, bandwidth, and hardware and software requirements. This is important background information to know in case you are asked, but only if you are asked. Otherwise, concentrate on the big picture: how many people will be affected and how much will it cost.
- *Don't promise to save money.* A common misconception of legislators—deriving, no doubt, from wishful thinking—is that the Internet will save government

great sums of money. This has rarely, if ever, been the case, at least as far as library services go. A better case to be made is that the Internet will broaden access to resources, ensure access to people who currently do not have access, or allow more institutions to participate in access than would otherwise be possible. This is the case that was made with success by both the TexShare program in Texas and the GALILEO project in Georgia. Legislators in those states were never told that they would save money, but that the money that they would spend would leverage broader participation for the price.

- *Have a plan.* Sooner or later, an elected official will ask you if you have a plan. This is another way of asking you if you have a larger vision and long-term goals. This is not a bad question and, in fact, is the sort of thing that should have already taken place at the statewide level—in the library association, the state library, or both—prior to talking to the legislator. It is helpful to know how you will build out service on the long term with benchmark goals for each year of the plan. This tells the elected official that the project is sustainable, and that their money is well-spent with a cumulative effect beyond the current year.

- *Expect the unexpected question.* Sooner or later, you will be sitting in a legislator's office or, worse, in a committee hearing and get a question that seems to have nothing whatever to do with what you are pitching. Sometimes these questions can be anticipated, such as the inevitable Internet filtering question. But other times, these questions will be more unpredictable, such as your opinion of fees for library service, or a question about local taxing patterns, or anything else. It is a good idea to try to anticipate the question, then provide an answer as truthfully and quickly as possible, then move on.

- *Know the legislator.* If the person you are talking to introduced the bill on Internet filtering, there is not much point in trying to talk them out of supporting that bill. What committees are they on? What types of bills have they introduced? How are they regarded by their colleagues? Who co-sponsors their bills? What institutions in their district will be affected? These are all questions you should know before you approach your legislator.

THE TRICK QUESTIONS

There is nothing you can do to guard against all trick questions. But there are some questions that come up so often that a library advocate would be foolish not to have a reply ready. Remember, these questions can come up in any library context and are not limited to discussions of Internet. These questions are typical:

- Do you allow children to view Internet pornography in your library?
- How do you propose that we protect against pedophiles that stalk children in chat rooms?
- You don't buy pornography for your library collection, why should you buy it on the Internet?
- I think we should charge the public to use the Internet in libraries, don't you?

- Why are you back here again this year, we paid for all the libraries to be connected last year.
- You're not still buying books, are you? Everything you need is on the Internet.
- I read an article that the Internet is going to make libraries obsolete. Is that true?
- Do you have e-books in your library?
- Why should we keep building libraries when people can dial in from home and get all the information they need?
- I went to webhelp.com and got an answer to a question from a live operator for free in less than five minutes without leaving my house. Can your library do that?

You can have answers ready for these predictable questions, but you cannot guard against every question. If you get a question you are not prepared for, it is always okay to say, "I don't have that answer, but I can get it for you."

KEYS TO SELLING YOUR IDEA

Keeping in mind the motivating factors mentioned above, test your Internet proposal to determine if you can promise any of the following points. It isn't necessarily fatal if you can't, but it will certainly help if it does:

- Provide access to persons that would not otherwise have access
- Expand service to a great number of new users
- Allow the leveraging of assets (such as occurs with collective purchasing options)

- Represent a demonstrable service upgrade for library users in the legislator's home district and elsewhere
- Concentrate on funding in one-time, fixed costs rather than ongoing costs such as staff or telecommunications
- Introduce an interesting new service for a reasonable cost
- Be part of a long-term plan that ensures that the public investment in hardware and software will not be immediately obsolete.

Just be sure that if you promise any of these points, you can deliver if challenged. Have key facts memorized or at your fingertips and be sure that what you are telling your legislator is accurate information. Don't guess—you could lose your credibility if you turn out to be too far off the mark.

FORMULATING THE MESSAGE

Obviously, it is advisable to prepare and review ahead of time materials that formulate your message. This will help you get your story straight, anticipate questions, and hone your arguments. Before embarking upon writing these materials, you should check to see what materials your state library association has already prepared so that you do not have to reinvent these materials and arguments.

You will not always have the same length of time to present arguments to elected officials (when the legislature is recessed you may have long interviews with your representatives, while in the in session you may only get a couple of minutes while walking down the hall). For this reason, you may find it helpful to have three levels of message formulated as follows:

1. *The one-pager.* This is the standard position paper and presents a relatively lengthy statement of background, problem, and proposed solution. This is where you develop your idea in more fully articulated statements that can be presented to the legislator with background materials attached. If you are lucky, the legislator and the aides will skim this material and keep it on hand as background.
2. *Issue in brief.* This presents the issue you are advocating in a one-paragraph format. This can be included in a letter or fax to the representative, in published materials, or presented with other issues.
3. *Soundbite.* This is a one-sentence statement of the issue presented in a way that will grab attention and throw a bright light on the needs addressed. Often a piece of statistical data is useful in such a statement, provided it is comprehensible, irrefutable, and highly persuasive. Such statements can be presented in brief interviews with elected officials and the press.

CONCLUSION

Working with elected officials is a tricky process because of the political minefield through which you have to tread. This is particularly difficult when controversial issues are being discussed. With some preparation and foresight, you can tailor a message that will demonstrate how the proposal helps library users in the legislator's district and beyond. There is still a great deal of work to be done to ensure that we have the library service of all types—traditional as well as electronic—that our communities need.

Chapter 9

Working with Staff to Convey a Uniform Message

Carolyn Caywood

Without a clearly stated and readily available policy on Internet use in the library, staff cannot consistently handle the complex issues that are inevitable. It is human nature to deduce rules from what seems to be accepted behavior and to attempt to apply those deductions in new situations. Each individual, however, sees events through a personal perspective and draws slightly different conclusions. Though no policy can cover all the possibilities inventive library patrons will come up with, a policy can add the library's philosophical context to the staff member's perceptions and make consistency possible.

Even so, staff must have confidence in a policy for it to be effective. When a rule doesn't make sense to people, they begin to reinterpret it, and pretty soon verbal versions passed on to new employees and the public vary from the written document. Involving staff in the development of the policy can prevent this by making sure that their concerns are addressed and by highlighting areas where additional training will help staff understand and implement the reasoning behind the rule. In their preface to *Model Policies for Small and Medium Public Libraries*, Jeanette Larson and Herman L. Totten remind policy developers, "They [policies] should be the result of input and review by others who are affected by the policies or who must carry them out or support them" (Larson and Totten, 1998:xi).

STAFF INPUT AND REVIEW

Policy decisions must be both correct and acceptable. For a library policy, correct means abiding by the law and the profession's philosophy. Acceptable means that those who are affected by the policy believe it is reasonable. Because acceptability is crucial to policy effectiveness, the process of policy development is equally as important as the resulting document and must be planned with care. Those who provide input deserve response. While not every issue raised will be echoed in the policy, some can help shape training or public relations.

Look for ways to involve as many staff as possible in the process of policy development. Depending on the resources of the institution, different teams can work on:

- Gathering and analyzing staff input
- Reviewing existing policy documents for Internet implications

- Evaluating technology, furnishings, and building lay-out
- Training
- Public relations
- Overall coordination of these group efforts

A non-judgmental forum for input, like brainstorming, is an effective starting point for policy development. If a catalyst is needed, try providing a "log" of possible uses of an Internet workstation over a day's time such as that shown on page 155. Ask staff for both their own concerns and what they've heard from patrons. In a system with several facilities, each may have a different perspective on the issues because of physical building constraints, staff resources, institutional cultures, and differing mixes of patrons. Offer some form of individual input as well for those who aren't as comfortable expressing opinions in a group and for ideas that arise on reflection after the discussion. A process of ranking will also be informative. While many of their concerns might be predicted, the way staff prioritize them may not be so obvious.

Once a policy is drafted, send it out to staff for review, along with proposals for training and publicizing and any other plans that have grown out of staff input. Staff will be particularly sensitive to the tone of the policy since they will need to use its language. Barbara Jones, in *Libraries, Access, and Intellectual Freedom: Developing Policies for Public and Academic Libraries,* describes the roles of "strategy, style and substance" in a policy (Jones, 1999:96). Style can be judged by asking staff if they would feel good about quoting from the policy. Most staff will identify jargon, vague wordings or passive constructions that leave responsibility unclear, and lists of thou-shalt-nots as barriers to communication with the public. Jones observes, "There are never any guarantees, but good faith attempts to link regulations to positive outcomes—like enhanced library service—tend to be looked on more kindly by courts and the general public alike than seemingly arbitrary and disconnected rules" (Ibid:13).

Finally, staff need a mechanism for reporting when circumstances call for policy revision. Larson and Totten offer a diagram of "The Life Cycle of Library Policy" showing that the process is circular. All policies should be evaluated on a regular schedule, but given the rapidity with which new aspects of the Internet appear, staff will probably be the first to notice unanticipated behaviors and thus drive the cycle on its next revolution.

INSTITUTIONAL VALUES

Implicit in staff involvement in policy development is the presumption that staff are valued by the library for their expertise and community contacts. As we move into an information economy, other organizations are discovering what libraries should have known all along—that knowledge workers are just as important as capital assets. In *Engines of Prosperity: Templates for the Information Age*, Geraldo R. Ungson and John D. Trudel assert that, "The Machine Age 'language of business' (traditional accounting) is poorly suited to managing knowledge. People are assets, not expenses" (Ungson and Trudel, 1998:37). One of the benefits the Internet offers libraries is the opportunity to highlight the importance of knowledgeable staff to patrons and funding authorities. Nevertheless, the value staff add to the organization is dependent on their understanding of the organization's mission and their confidence in the reasoning behind decisions.

Staff who lack that understanding or confidence may react by hiding behind policy. Using policy as a shield rather than a guide can also indicate a climate of fear where problems are solved by assigning blame. Or, it can be a symptom of belief that the policy is not really in the public's best interest. It may mean that the library has not invested sufficiently in effective training to enable staff to act with confidence. These kinds of staff insecurity are completely incompatible with assisting patrons in Internet use. The American Family Association video *Excess Access: Are Your Children Safe in the Public Library?* vividly demonstrates how hiding behind policy appears to the public.

The way the library as an organization views its staff will determine how well they are able to help patrons. If a library does not trust and value its staff, neither the institution nor the staff are likely to trust library patrons. As a result, its policies will tend toward an endless multiplication of ever more detailed restrictions that defeat its purpose, consume its staff resources, and drive off patrons. Here are some questions that may clarify institutional values.

- Is exploring the whole range of human knowledge and opinion recognized as relevant to library work?
- Are staff consulted as knowledgeable resources?
- Is staff training seen as an investment that adds value to library service?
- What decisions are staff empowered to make without referral to authority?

- Are policies based on the premise that staff do the best they know how?

A library that remembers its purpose in adding Internet access is to increase knowledge and understanding, that invests in its staff and then trusts them to carry out that purpose, has laid the foundation for public acceptance of its policy decisions.

POLICY CONTEXTS

An Internet policy must function in contexts ranging from technology to community and law to library mission. Staff confidence depends on knowing that the policy is solidly based in the reality of these contexts. Staff want to see evidence that the policy writers understand the technology. If part of the policy is contingent on software functionality, involving staff in its testing can relieve anxiety. The resources of the organization—layout of facilities, type and quantity of equipment, and staff time and training—also shape the environment in which staff will have to implement the policy. Safety of staff and patrons should always be a priority, but since many of the concerns about the Internet are framed in terms of safety, this is a good time to review procedures for handling dangerous situations and verify that the building has been made as safe as possible.

The peculiarities of the library's community and the demographics of library patrons are another policy context. Staff can report the kinds of school assignments that will impact Internet use, the proportion of patrons who are fearful of computers, and how often visitors come seeking access to their home e-mail. They will know whether letters to the newspaper reflect widespread opinion.

The Internet policy must fit into the framework of the library's mission and its other policies. This is part of the strategy Jones advocates: "Strategic policy entails a careful linking of the policy to the library's mission, rather than presenting it simply as an idealistic document with no perceived connection to reality" (Jones:96). Staff and patrons look for a consistent philosophy across rules. Citing and cross-referencing other library policies helps to show that the Internet is not something apart from other library services.

Ideally, the mission would be obvious from the policies and each policy an integral part of the total library picture. It may be, however, that the library's current mission statement is not worded in a way that easily accommodates Internet access and it is time for a revision. Other policies, too, may suddenly seem jarringly outdated. If so, revision must be a priority because the library's mission and all its policies need to make sense together if the Internet policy is to be implemented effectively.

All library staff need to understand the philosophical background of library services. Staff also need to be aware of legislation and court decisions that affect the policy and understand the legal constraints on library authority. Knowing that the policy has had legal review will contribute to staff peace of mind. While professional staff have presumably been exposed to library principles, they still need to understand their application in their own library. And staff who have not studied library sciences are, nevertheless, ambassadors to the community with whom they will share their understanding, or lack of it.

TYPICAL STAFF CONCERNS

Many of the issues the Internet raises are exacerbated by their impact on the amount of staff time available to deal with them. Anything computer-related still seems to come with the myth of saving time when in reality computers almost always take more time because they create new possibilities. And, those new possibilities create unfamiliar situations where staff must figure out how policy applies.

Staff will want to know what new tasks they are taking on and how they are expected to prioritize them. The extent to which they are expected to troubleshoot technical problems or teach the mechanics of using a computer will affect how much time is left to guide a search or explain library policy. Conversely, an out-of-order computer waiting for repair increases demand for those that remain.

In most libraries demand for Internet access exceeds the available computers—even when all are working—and staff must allocate this limited resource fairly. It is crucial that everyone feels that the process is fair and that the process is respectful of staff time and of user convenience and confidentiality. No staff member wants to spend the day arbitrating disputes over whose turn it is to use the Internet workstation. Building layout and workstation design can also save or waste staff time.

Even in communities where many patrons are familiar with computers and the Internet, there will still be those who have to start from scratch. Often patrons who would be happy to rely on staff to do their searching in other media tend to think they ought to learn to use the Internet. Conversely, those who are accustomed to surfing may still have little idea how to construct a successful search and may find the library's configuration of options and preferences unfamiliar. All this adds up to the need for staff to do a lot more one-on-one training than was needed in the past. Training aids, from handouts and help screens to volunteers and classes, may not be mentioned in the policy but will help alleviate anxieties about implementing it.

Staff need to know what patron behaviors are not acceptable and how staff are expected to address them. Their level of authority and responsibility needs to be made as clear as possible. If there is an existing policy on patron behavior, most situations may already be covered. Behavior rules should make clear how the behavior disrupts library use, not focus on the cause. For example, it is the disturbance of readers that is at issue, whether a baby is crying, a cell phone is ringing, or someone is loudly sharing an Internet discovery. Some behavior rules are made necessary by poor building design, so any improvements that can reduce the number of rules staff have to enforce will free more time for staff to assist patrons. Behavior rules should always have a demonstrable connection to improving everyone's ability to use the library and should be enforceable without requiring staff to snoop or otherwise violate library principles or the law.

Since some behaviors are illegal, everyone will be more comfortable knowing that local law enforcement is familiar with the library's policies and prepared to respond appropriately. Staff should know when and how to report an incident to the police and what to expect from them. Both staff and police need to be aware that decisions about the legality of content belong to the courts.

Nevertheless there will be situations when staff must use

judgement and discretion in the face of ambiguity. In doing so, they must, as ALA's *Code of Ethics* (1995) says, distinguish between personal convictions and professional duties. Just as staff want to know the extent of their authority, they want assurance that they can refer a problem to someone else if it is beyond their ability to handle. While a staff member's beliefs or taste cannot limit library service, the library should be prepared to protect a staff member from harassment. In *Libraries, the First Amendment and Cyberspace: What You Need to Know*, Robert S. Peck explains the legal issues that apply to library staff who might be harassed (Peck, 2000).

STAFF TRAINING

The need for various kinds of training will be obvious to staff. Even if they are comfortable with managing behavior problems, a review with application to Internet situations will be reassuring. Staff need to feel confident of their online searching skills and their ability to solve common technical problems. Teaching patrons quickly and pleasantly is another skill that's too often left to chance and individual personality. Of course, the policy itself requires its own training so that staff feel able to discuss its application to an individual patron's desires.

These topics cannot be adequately conveyed by lecturing; they require time for practicing with various situations. A training Website with searching exercises can increase staff skills, help them discover potential difficulties, and allow time to simply explore the Internet. Role-playing exercises let staff rehearse their responses to specific situations and may reveal points that are not clear. Dramatizing how not to respond can relieve tensions and create learning through discussion. Possible scenarios to explore include responding to:

- A neophyte's request for help
- A shopper concerned about privacy
- A patron who has encountered unexpected, unpleasant content
- A patron concerned about what some other patron is viewing
- A group of patrons surfing together noisily
- A patron concerned about his or her child's safety
- A patron who is convinced everything can be found on the Internet
- A patron who isn't finished when his or her time is up
- A patron who asks about filters
- A patron who persists in asking for help with content that is disturbing to the staff member.

Staff can suggest other scenarios depending on the specifics of the library's policy and on their own concerns. Responses should reveal that staff's reference interview skills and knowledge of good search strategies can resolve many situations.

PUBLIC RELATIONS

Each day, as staff explain and apply the policy to patrons, they are engaged in public relations. Their own feelings about the policy will affect the public's reaction. Their ability to express its rationale in their own words and through their actions will have more effect than press releases and ribbon cuttings. If they are confident that they understand the policy, they can use it as a guide to find ways to satisfy legitimate patron needs. If, on the other hand, the policy is most frequently cited as a reason for saying no, both it and the library will drop in public esteem.

Message points can help staff connect their work with each patron back to the policy. Opportunities exist in patron transactions to reinforce the following ideas:

- Internet access fits the library mission; it amplifies but does not replace traditional library services.
- Knowledgeable staff make Internet use in the library more efficient and successful than access at home or at a web cafe.
- Staff care about children. They are ready to offer help to families when asked, but don't want to intrude on parental prerogatives. They want parents to understand what can be expected of the library and the Internet so children are not endangered through false assumptions.
- The policy has been developed through thorough consideration to enhance the benefits of Internet access for library patrons.

While these daily interactions are the foundation of library public relations, staff and administration both will probably be more comfortable having official statements come from a designated spokesperson. Staff will particularly want to know how to respond to reporters seeking pictures or patron interviews in the library. The process of making a referral to a spokesperson should convey a desire to provide more information, not an attempt to dodge hard questions. Like other information referrals, having the staff member set up the contact avoids misunderstanding. Using the reference interview process can defuse what could be a potentially hostile situation while keeping the interaction in a context where staff are confident of their skills.

SUMMARY

The goal in working with the staff is to build their understanding and confidence so they can implement the policy consistently in ways that help patrons accept that the policy is in their best interest. If this goal is to be achieved, staff need to be involved in the development of the policy and in planning for its implementation. The library needs to take advantage of staff's knowledge and invest in meeting their needs. Staff must understand policy decisions and believe the policy is practical and fits the library's philosophical framework. The anarchy of the Internet creates a minefield for organizations committed to rigid rules and authoritarian structures. To implement Internet access successfully, a library must be able to trust its staff and staff must trust their institution and colleagues.

REFERENCES

American Family Association. 2000. *Excess Access: Are Your Children Safe in the Public Library?* [Video].

American Library Association. 1995. *American Library Association Code of Ethics.* Chicago: ALA. Available: *www.ala.org/alaorg/oif/ethics.html.*

Jones, Barbara M. 1999. *Libraries, Access, and Intellectual Freedom: Developing Policies for Public and Academic Libraries.* Chicago: ALA.

Larson, Jeanette and Herman L. Totten. 1998. *Model Policies for Small and Medium Public Libraries.* New York: Neal-Schuman.

Peck, Robert S. 2000. *Libraries, the First Amendment and Cyberspace: What You Need to Know.* Chicago: ALA.

Ungson, Geraldo R. and John D. Trudel. 1998. *Engines of Prosperity: Templates for the Information Age.* London: Imperial College Press.

Log of a library public access Internet workstation

Consider how these Internet activities might relate to the library's policy:

10:00 a.m.   Grandmother asks staff how to enter URL of family's Website to see photos of new baby.

10:10 a.m.   Tourist telnets to home Internet account to read e-mail.

10:40 a.m.   New resident prints out California state income tax forms.

10:55 a.m.   While browsing Websites on corgis, a dog owner uses a mail-to link to alert the Webmaster to out-of-date and broken links.

11:10 a.m.   A customer who has heard of Hotmail, but who has no computer at home, asks staff how to set up free personal e-mail account through the Hotmail Website.

11:25 a.m.   After staff identify a patron's favorite childhood book and show the patron a used book dealer's Website, his wife uses her credit card to order copy of book.

11:35 a.m.   New user fills in online library survey form.

11:45 a.m.   Genealogist researches maternal grandmother's maiden name.

12:10 p.m.   After checking NADA, seller posts ad for used motorcycle to local newsgroups.

12:20 p.m.   Customer repeatedly asks staff for help printing sexually explicit pictures.

12:40 p.m.   After browsing virtual greeting card Websites, a customer selects and mails birthday card.

12:45 p.m.   A borrower looks up an author in catalog, discovering a link to the author's Website where he leaves a note demanding an explanation for why the author killed off the heroine in his latest book.

12:55 p.m.	An investor checks stock quotes, then uses her cell phone to place sell order.
1:15 p.m.	Local history buff searches on "French Lick" and gets 8,600 matches, some with sexually explicit content, then asks the staff for explanation.
1:30 p.m.	Voter asks for help on how to ftp the text of a bill from a Congressional Website.
1:45 p.m.	Window-shopper browses the e-Bay Website.
2:15 p.m.	Reporter asks staff if they will agree to be filmed locating "cyberporn" on the Internet.
2:30 p.m.	Nature lover takes virtual tour of swamp preserve in Florida.
2:45 p.m.	Optimist surfs gambling Websites and decides to place a bet on the Swiss Lotto.
3:00 p.m.	New user asks for basic introduction to use of the Web browser.
3:25 p.m.	Political activist finds torture victim's photo and saves as wallpaper for the next user's edification.
3:30 p.m.	After recovering from the above, a movie fan types "McGuffin" into search engine to find a definition of this term.
3:35 p.m.	Student fills out registration form on the *Time* Website so that she can read article.
3:50 p.m.	Teen logs onto a chat room to talk to friend at the next workstation.
4:20 p.m.	Adventure enthusiast goes to xyzzy.com to play a game called Colossal Cave.
4:50 p.m.	Music lover listens to newest release from favorite rap group.
4:55 p.m.	Student downloads and pastes pictures from Website into report on floppy.

5:10 p.m.	Traveler browses bed and breakfast Websites and makes reservation for weekend.
5:20 p.m.	Gardener searches for recipes that will help use up an excess of zucchinis.
5:35 p.m.	Child browses candy company Websites and enters contest, giving name of school, grade and teacher.
5:45 p.m.	Browser watches "webcam" of fish swimming around in aquarium.
6:00 p.m.	Staff discover that a customer has found *Alice in Wonderland* online and hit the Print button.
6:05 p.m.	Hacker-wannabe brags to friends he can find out what previous users did by looking at browser history file.
6:10 p.m.	French student browses Websites in France for language practice.
6:25 p.m.	Student asks how to find the assignment his teacher put up on the school's Website.
6:30 p.m.	Man asks child passing by if she'd like to look at some "pretty pictures."
6:40 p.m.	Student practices on virtual frog dissection Website.
6:58 p.m.	Participant shows up for the 7 p.m. IRC book discussion hosted by another public library, but all computers are in use.
7:30 p.m.	Collector appraises her Beanie Babies by checking prices on the Web.
7:45 p.m.	Kid asks for help with perpetual calendar to find out on what day of week Columbus sighted land.
7:55 p.m.	Poet uploads latest effort to an online literary magazine.
8:10 p.m.	Student asks how to find those Websites that offer recycled term papers.

8:20 p.m.	Home buyer browses real estate listings and makes appointments for weekend visits.
8:50 p.m.	Teen uses dad's credit card number to access www.whorehouse.com.
8:55 p.m.	Staff shut down equipment for the night.

Chapter 10

Ethics and the Internet

Susan Fuller

A librarian is deciding whether to place a particular link on the library's list of suggested sites for teenagers. The site in question is a subject of great interest to local high school students but also of great concern to some of their parents. Will the governing board support her action? A high school librarian in California sends his students to the public library because the filters in the school library block students from material they need. A library board is confronted with frightened parents, worried that their junior high school students can access the Ku Klux Klan Website. Another hears from parents unhappy that the library has restricted chat room use. Their son finds chat rooms entertaining and they believe he has good judgment.

When a library governing board tries to make policy around these kinds of issues they are often in a maze of emotion, pressure, and conflict. How are the decisions

made? Even if there are policies in place, the board can
be whipsawed by the volatility of the situation. The temp-
tation to do something injudicious just to make it go away
is overwhelming.

The Internet presents difficult issues for all kinds of libraries. In this article I will present the ethical issues surrounding use of the Internet in libraries and how those
issues were addressed and resolved in the Santa Clara
County Library.

INTERNET HAS RAISED THE STAKES AND VISIBILITY OF THE FIRST AMENDMENT IN PUBLIC LIBRARIES

Controversies about ideas in library collections are not
new, but with the introduction of the Internet, they have
become far more intense and public. More than ever, governing boards need a decision-making process that relies
on logic and reason, rather than one that reacts to political pressure.

It is remarkable that the Internet, the same instrument
that has made it possible for us to fulfill our information
mission so successfully, should be the tool that also makes
us so vulnerable. Across the country, in numerous communities, librarians are struggling with decisions about
how to best use the Internet, both the bright and the dark
side of it. Librarians are not making those decisions alone.
While in the past the community may have been only pe-
ripherally interested, now there is a sense of urgency and
an opinion about the library's moral imperative. If the activists' positions are not adopted, major confrontations can

ensue. Librarians and their governing boards have two challenges. One is to understand why the Internet has become such a political fireball. The other is to find a process that will lead to wise decisions.

STEREOTYPES, MEMORIES, AND ASSUMPTIONS

Internet in public libraries has been one of the hottest talk show and legislative issues around. Understanding why may help organizations find the road out of what can be a morass.

People are often surprised when the library becomes a political firestorm. The stereotype that we know so well leads to an expectation of a quiet, protected, regulated, and safe place. A place thought of with fondness and nostalgia, not an institution that is igniting one of the most controversial issues of our time.

The public library occupies a very special niche in the affections of many people. Embedded in warm remembrances are the memories of our first reach toward independence and a sense of doing so in a safe environment. Maybe we felt safe because our stereotype of the librarian as a protector helped cushion the anxiety engendered by new and challenging ideas, concepts that might have been outside the framework of acceptability in our own families. In those new ideas we found a confirmation of ourselves as individuals.

As we moved into adulthood, the personal feeling we had for the library remained. In fact, most people think of the library in quite parochial and personal terms. In surveys, people talk about special experiences like bringing children to storytime, enjoying browsing the resources or finding refuge from stress in a good book. The library is an individual and self-centered experience. The library doesn't feel controversial because our affection for the institution and our experience with it leads us to expect that the institution is us and reflects all our ideas, values, standards, and hopes.

WE DO NOT ALL SHARE THE SAME VIEWS

For most, the experience of finding disturbing ideas in the library is still cloaked with the positive feelings they always held about the institution. For others, it can come as a visceral shock to realize that ideas in the library's collection reflect other values as well as their own, values that seem totally repugnant to them. Most of us have an emotional assumption (even if our intellect tells us otherwise) that what seems wrong to us will seem equally wrong to others. Everyone carries in his head a definition of what is "inappropriate." Librarians hear this all the time when an upset patron says, "No one could approve of that!" or "I'm not a censor, but . . ." We give lip service to intellectual diversity and tolerance but our natural inclination is to believe that everyone is "like us."

"Like us" means sharing our perception about what is safe, our ideas about what should be seen and by whom, our convictions about how children should be raised and educated, our beliefs about what is sacred and profane. It can feel like a personal betrayal when the public library does not meet these expectations. Actually, our communities are diverse and the points of view held by people are many. The very essence of the American experience is an affirmation of each individual's right to hold, receive, and express their own viewpoint.

The public library's role as a public forum often runs squarely counter to concerns about unsafe ideas. The prevailing conception of the library is certain to conflict with the reality of the library's purpose. When people think of the library as an extension of their own living rooms it is very difficult for them to understand the argument that the library is a proving ground for the First Amendment and a place where people are not safe from ideas or from the responsibility to decide what ideas to pursue.

FEAR OF NEW TECHNOLOGIES

While there have always been discussions about the suitability of certain ideas in the library, the Internet definitely increases the heat of those discussions. Concern about expression has often centered on new technology. Technology changes our perceptions of the givens in the world. Think about the implications of the printing press or, closer to our time, the automobile, television, radio, or the movies. All these technologies made it much less possible for us to remain isolated from a world that does not share our values. Restriction is a way to control change that we don't understand and fear.

LIBRARY SELECTION MEANS "SAFE" AND "GOOD"

Changes brought by the Internet have caused a revolution in the way we think about our place in the world. In only a few years our entire relationship to information has changed. In the past, without a great deal of trouble, we only got information because someone—a publisher, television or radio network, or a recording company—decided to place it in the public purview. Further, when we got that information, it was vetted, or at least we thought it was, just as we thought we were protected in the public library.

Now, anyone, anywhere with a modicum of technical skill can place information on the Web. Every hour, thousands of individuals do just that. Most likely there is no intermediary and no one to verify that information is correct or even to certify its source.

When libraries offer access to the Internet they offer a resource that is a connection point where everything is available. The connection is the selection. There is no way libraries could (even if they should) review or endorse all the sites. People who believe that the library puts a "Seal of Approval" on everything in the collection are especially troubled by this issue. The notion that our relationship to information has become personal and cannot be centrally controlled is empowering but can also be very threatening.

When people are threatened and frightened they retreat to a place where they can be in charge. It is not surprising that the unease and uncertainty expressed about the Internet is manifested in an arena where individuals feel they do have some control, the public library.

SOCIETAL VALUES IN CONFLICT

Battles over Internet access in the library mirror deep societal differences. The questions revolve around several points. What is "responsible" behavior and who should define and enforce it? What is appropriate action when it comes to minors? It is important to think about these two issues before beginning to craft any process that can hope to lead to a satisfactory resolution.

MINORS

Fear about a lack of values and bad ideas usually centers around our concerns about children. As a society we can find common ground in our commitment that children should be safe. We want them to learn how to evaluate ideas, make good decisions, and become responsible, happy adults.

It is when we talk about how that can happen that we find deep differences. To begin, what do we mean by minors? Often in community discussions the picture of the child who could be harmed varies considerably. Do we think that a five- and fifteen-year-old have the same level of judgment and maturity? Is every thirteen-year-old the same? The law defines a minor as one under the age of eighteen. Is that the standard to use?

This discussion is made even more complex because there is no clear enumeration of a minor's rights to information. While it is clear that adults have a constitutional right to legal speech, there has not been a definitive Supreme Court case defining the rights of minors (though there is at least one lower court case pending that may resolve these issues). There are certainly some cases that establish certain information rights for minors. However, there is no case that definitively draws the distinction between a seventeen-year-old's right to information and the guardian prerogatives of his parents.

WHOSE VALUES PREVAIL?

When these disagreements arise we try to find common ground in values. Society agrees that values are important and that they define both our world view and our relationship to others. But what world view? When there is disagreement, who should make the choice? Should values be determined by a majority vote? Should the government be the arbiter? What is the role of the individual, the child, the parent, the government?

On a practical level, the discussion often centers around behavior. The popular notion that the village should be responsible for socially acceptable conduct may be appropriate in the case of theft, physical assault, and murder. However, the regulation of thought is another matter. The Constitution charges the government to protect individual inquiry.

As we begin to try to respond to these issues in our communities we must remember that these are not solely library issues. We can find better solutions if we treat the concerns in their broadest context, as concerns and questions of the entire society.

A parent in Santa Clara County made this point when she said "Moves to protect minors may be, in some sense, moves to protect our own innocence about the depth of change in our own society. Access in the library will become a side issue. We can take a narrow approach and appear safe, but we should rather focus on teaching children necessary moral and critical thinking skills to avoid bad influence from the increasingly available information."

This parent understands the complexity of this issue and the difficulty of finding easy solutions that reduce the polarization of opinion.

EXPERIENCE IN SANTA CLARA COUNTY LIBRARY

The struggle with the issue of Internet access in Santa Clara County Library lasted almost two years. A group of parents challenged the library's policy and requested that minors' access to the Internet be restricted. The library's governing board, nine local city councils, and various other bodies held many public hearings. Local and national press attention was constant. Television, radio, and print reporters became regular visitors to my office and to the libraries where staff were also interviewed at length. Discussion was polarized and bitter. Virtually all other business stopped as the fire of their impassioned opinions consumed all the players.

Although the intensity and emotion of the discussion escalated rapidly, the library's governing board resisted making a quick decision. They realized that a good decision had to involve all the stakeholders. It was also clear that they had to find a way to reestablish trust and bring the discussion back to judicious examination from its highly pitched rhetoric.

To further complicate the board's task, the library has a very inclusive system of governance. Nine city council members and two members of the Board of Supervisors sit on the governing board. Behind the board stand 52 other elected officials from each of the jurisdictions. All 63 elected officials have a direct sense of ownership and participation in the governance of the County Library.

Fifty additional people participate in eight citizen commissions, advisory bodies appointed by each city council. Each community library also has a Friends of the Library group. In all, there are more than one hundred individuals who have a direct, structural relationship to the library. All those people not only have a place to give input and direction, they also do it. The comments of all of them were crucial as the governing board struggled to define the library's values and recognize the views of all the stakeholders.

Clearly, it would not be possible to find a good solution without a sound process of decision making. The board and the library decided to hire the Markkula Center for Applied Ethics at Santa Clara University to help chart a sound course of action.

The Markkula Center for Applied Ethics and Thomas Shanks

The Center and its then-director Thomas Shanks, SJ works with business and public organizations to create an ethical lens for thoughtful decision making, particularly in highly contentious situations. Ethics means making decisions consistent with the values of the organization. The process includes defining the organization's values, including the concerns of all stakeholders, asking questions about the consequences of decisions, and matching the results with the organization's goals. Dr. Shanks was charged with helping the library board develop a process and identify criteria for making a decision. He was not asked to develop or recommend a solution.

The ethics model

The ethics model asks that organizations look at themselves and determine what kind of an organization they choose to be. "What are we like when we are at our best?" is the question Dr. Shanks poses. This question and the ethics model was very helpful to Santa Clara County Library as it floundered in the midst of a bitter censorship battle. In collaboration with Shanks, stakeholders within the aegis of Santa Clara County Library came to agreement on values and found a workable solution to the Internet access question.

Key facts about the Santa Clara County Library

Santa Clara County Library serves a suburban population of 400,000 in nine cities and the unincorporated area of the area known to the world as Silicon Valley. Many of the most famous names in the computer world and their employees—both rank-and-file and chief executives—live in the library's service area. The number of members of the public with ties to the Internet is very high. Library use is very high as well with one of the highest per capita use rates in the nation. Use has grown almost 60 percent over the past five years.

The library has a strong collection and an ongoing commitment to electronic resources. At the time of the initial protest, graphical Internet access had been in place for almost a year and there had been tremendous public response. The very few incidents involving use of the Internet by minors have nearly all been about disruption caused by noisy students congregating at a machine rather than content-based problems.

At the time of the initial complaint, the library had about 250 computers with text or graphical Internet access. Behavior guidelines had been established to ensure individual privacy. In addition, the library had created tools and begun training programs for families and people of all ages to help promote computer literacy and safe online use.

The library's policy for many years has been one of individual responsibility. The library provides the broadest range of resources possible and patrons are expected to decide how to use the resources in ways that meet their needs. Parents of minors are expected to set guidelines for their children. Library staff do not monitor individual family decisions.

Developing the solution

As the library board began to work with Dr. Shanks, they first asked him to create a neutral place where all stakeholders were identified and had a chance to state their views. Dr. Shanks held a series of group and individual meetings and also did some additional research. This information was compiled into a report for the board and is available online at *www.scu.edu/ethics*.

At the same time Dr. Shanks was examining the issue,

staff were also reviewing and evaluating potential courses of action. Several extensive staff reports were created for the board. Many private citizens with opinions to express took advantage of an extensive array of public hearings and their comments were compiled. Using the Markkula findings, staff reports, and the opinions expressed in the hearing and by mail, the board began to identify the stakeholders and issues that had to be considered.

The stakeholders

Santa Clara County Libraries are the cultural center of their communities. Understandably, many people were concerned about how access to this core institution would be regulated. Initially, the key players were the parents lodging the complaint and the discussion was a confrontation between them, the staff, and the board. Until Dr. Shanks began his work, it was hard for the board to keep the issues from being framed by the complainants.

As the discussion progressed other stakeholders emerged. Minors themselves began to be heard. In hearings, in the media, and in private and group discussions, some young people expressed their opinions. Although their wishes were not generally sought, the participation of a few well-spoken teenagers helped the board understand that minors are not all the same. A more active approach in seeking the opinion of this group could have been illuminating. The board may not have always understood the viewpoint of those they were seeking to protect.

Several parents who spoke disagreed with those who wanted restriction. They felt that they, not the government, should be providing guidance and supervision for their children. They expressed their belief that children learn by guided experimentation and education. They were not in favor of pornography but felt that government control is not the answer to raising their own children to be responsible adults.

A difficult conflict arose between those who felt parents should deal only with their own children and those who felt that the entire community should be responsible for every child. There was also disagreement about whether minority viewpoints should be allowed. Some people believed strongly that morality is established by the community standard and that minority points of view are not acceptable. These individuals also assumed that their beliefs represented those of the majority.

Staff opinion and legal review

The library staff and their attorneys argued that the library is a limited public forum, a place the government has established for the receipt of expressive activity. Staff and counsel emphasized that the public forum has the strongest First Amendment protection. The Supreme Court ruling in the Communications Decency Act underlined that opinion. Staff believed and continue to believe that it is the library's legal and ethical duty to protect each individual's right to legal speech.

All stakeholders agreed that it was important to support children and parents. They were polarized in their views as to how to proceed.

Setting values in Santa Clara County Library

Under Dr. Shanks' ethics model, the board began to define their values. They agreed on several concepts that had to be included in a successful decision. One of the most important agreements was that the library's public forum status must be maintained. This meant that the solution had to be based on choice, not restriction. It also meant that staff would continue to be facilitators, not gatekeepers, of information. Staff would not monitor content.

The board also wanted to support families and especially to offer options that would allow parents with differing viewpoints a choice in guiding their children's use of the library. They stressed that the options would be choices, not mandates. The board recognized that the law defines minors as those under 18. However, they also wanted to acknowledge that there is a difference between teenagers and very young children.

The board had to decide if the Internet is different from other information in the library's collection and should be treated with another standard. They agreed that the Internet should be part of their general access policy but because of the extensive information potential of the Internet, the library should provide users with extra support in its use. They also agreed that it was important to fully disclose to users the potential of the Internet—that some material could be distasteful and even illegal, and the fact that that information is not endorsed by the library.

In establishing their goals, they recognized significant disagreement over the definition of pornography as well as a lack of understanding of the definition of legal speech, confusion over the legal information rights of minors and, certainly, genuine parental concern, both from those who favor restriction and those who do not.

The following were elements of the board's policy:

- *Filters*. The board agreed that when the library is at its best it protects individual rights, offers choices, supports families and other users, and is forthcoming about material in its collections. As a result, the board directed staff to install filtering software on the Internet access computers in the children's rooms. The board intended the software to filter only sexually explicit sites. Information about this option was placed in all the library's orientation material so that parents could instruct their children according to their own values and their view of their child's maturity. Staff would not monitor minors' use of machines and would not direct youth to use filtered machines.
- *Consent*. A consent screen was installed that must be read and acknowledged by all users. The text warns the user that material on the Internet is not endorsed by the library and that some sites may be distasteful and even may contain illegal speech that is not protected by the First Amendment.
- *Choice*. In addition, the board adopted the staff recommendation to offer a choice of filtered or unfiltered access on all Internet stations in the library outside of the children's room. This meant that anyone of any age could choose the approach that best suited his or her needs and values. Staff would not interfere in that choice.
- *Education*. The board also endorsed and encouraged the educational actions that the library offered including classes for families and individuals, Web page links on the library homepage for children and others with

particular interests, privacy screens, and behavior rules that ensured the privacy and comfort of all patrons.

The decision

This solution was implemented in July 1998 and the great majority of users have found it acceptable. The Library Board reviewed and reconfirmed its policy in the spring of 1999, and again in April 2000. The process chosen by the Santa Clara County Library governing board was not perfect and did not relieve the board from a painful, frustrating experience. However, using an ethics model that helped them move logically from a statement of organizational values to a values related outcome did help them make a thoughtful and stable decision.

Observations

Several important lessons were learned during this process. First, patience, though tiring, is a virtue. None of the parties would have accepted the eventual decision early. It took time to realize the need for thoughtful process and the Markkula Center was not engaged until several months into the dispute. In an issue as complex as this one, confused individuals need time to think and explore ideas. Patience brought a more thoughtful and more inclusive solution. In the end, choice was preserved and options were offered. A quick decision in the beginning would have tended to respond only to the extremes of both sides. Using the values model helped the Board to frame the issue in a more inclusive way. The way issues are framed is crucial to finding a good resolution. If a small but vocal minority is allowed to define the parameters of the discussion, it may be harder and perhaps impossible to find common ground.

In discussions as emotional as this one, creating a neutral space where all viewpoints can be heard is essential. Bringing the neutral credibility of Dr. Shanks and the Markkula Center into the process ensured that all perspectives could be considered and gave the board more control over the situation.

An enriching and gratifying outcome of the conflict was the strength and solidarity developed by the staff. It is impossible to overstate the stress experienced by library employees and to over-emphasize the sense of commitment and principle that they exhibited. Deputy County Librarian Julie Farnsworth, brand new in her job, gave tireless, compassionate support to employees and to the county librarian. Gilroy Community Librarian Lani Yoshimura, whose library was in the heart of the controversy, not only supported her own staff but offered an inspiring vision to the whole Library as well. In our support for the Board, our response to the politics of a tense situation and our constant restating of the vitality of the Library's mission, the staff stood as one.

Most important, the values process and the time allowed to the discussion gave the community an opportunity to talk and think about the public library in a way that they may never have done before. On reflection, many people came to support the library's neutral mission and its gift of self-actualization.

CONCLUSION

Faced with anger, discord, and fear, it is easy for a governing board to make quick, ill-considered decisions that are not responsive to the mission of the library or the needs of everyone who uses it. All of us who work in or govern a public library must remember that we are caretakers of an institution that guarantees a precious right of Americans, the right to know.

The public library is one of this country's most democratic forces. Those of us responsible for its care have the responsibility to be the voices of reason and conscience. Even when it is tedious, frustrating, or frightening, it is our privilege to preserve and enhance the public library through our most thoughtful and ethical decisions. It is worth our best efforts to achieve that goal.

Chapter 11

Introducing Internet Access in Schools: Strategies for Managing Controversy

M. Ellen Jay

PART I: OVERVIEW

Once the decision to provide in-school access to the Internet has been made, there are a number of technical issues that must be addressed. Initial decisions relate to the number and kind of computers to be acquired, purchase or lease agreements to be made, type of connection to be used, and physical placement throughout the school. While complicated and expensive, these technical decisions rarely generate the political controversy associated with the next round of decisions: those related to issues of access and supervision.

The ratio of computers to users will affect what is possible. A building with just a handful of access points and a large population of users will consider one set of management options, while a building with access points provided by labs, in classrooms, and the media center will need to consider another set. The age of the students will also obviously inform both sets of decisions.

Those responsible for making decisions related to access and supervision should carefully research and discuss a number of questions including:

1. What Internet protocols and services will students be allowed (or disallowed) to access? For example, will Web use be restricted to sites related to instruction or will students be able to surf freely? Will students have access to e-mail, chat rooms, and Newsgroups?
2. Will students be required to obtain a signed parental permission prior to using the Internet?
3. Will students be required to sign a code of ethics related to computer use?
4. Should the school establish a set of enforcement procedures and specify consequences for inappropriate use?
5. Will students be able to log on to the Internet independently or will staff participation be necessary?
6. Will passwords be required to access the Internet (or specific protocols)?
7. Will the school employ filtering software and/or other programs that regulate Internet use?
8. How will the school ensure equity of access time? Will there be limits on the duration of individual sessions?
9. Will the school place monitors in a way that facilitates adult supervision?

Although there is no one right and universal answer to these questions, successful management of Internet access issues does require that managers arrive at a staff consensus and seek community input during the decision making process.

No school will achieve long-term success in this arena unless it sends students a message from the beginning that they have a responsibility to use Internet access appropriately. Students should understand that if they should find themselves in an inappropriate site they do not stay there. Creating a climate in which students feel challenged to beat the system is a no-win situation for supervisory staff. Schools will achieve greater success if they partner with parents in sending this message. Internet use provides a real-life application for character education values.

Decisions related to providing training for staff and students are equally important. When the training component is overlooked, the investment in hardware and software is largely wasted. Administrators must motivate the instructional staff to use the technology. Staff need to develop the confidence to integrate use of computers into their instructional interactions. This requires a major change in teaching style, which is unlikely to happen without becoming a component of the teacher evaluation process.

Maintenance and system upgrade are also frequently overlooked. A quality program requires more ongoing attention than the initial equipment installation, policy decisions, and training. When administrators fail to provide adequate technical support staff to keep equipment up and running, consumable supplies to support printing, and eventual upgrade as equipment becomes outdated, the instructional program cannot prosper.

All of these decisions have budgetary implication. Internet access for a school requires a foundation of both short- and long-term financial planning. The quality of planning and decision making related to these basic issues will determine to a large extent the ease with which the instructional program integrates the use of the Internet. Even with the best planning, some degree of controversy will likely develop.

Understanding the medium

Much of the controversy related to student use of the Internet stems from misconceptions among parents and other community members about just what the Internet is. The Internet is thousands of networks linking schools, universities, businesses, government agencies, organizations, and individuals. No one owns it, and there are few, if any, regulations. As a result of the Internet's structure, anyone can post literally anything. In addition to sites that are obviously inappropriate for a school setting (e.g., sexually explicit sites), many other types of sites are intentionally misleading, inaccurate, and biased. Some sites are designed to appear to provide valid content when in fact they may actually be unsubstantiated opinion or manipulation. Without considerable experience in analyzing sites, student researchers can easily be misled. School library media specialists play an important role in helping students develop information literacy skills they need to make good decisions about Internet usage and evaluating information from the Internet. Successful management of the controversy surrounding children and the Internet is improved when schools let parents and other concerned community members know they are educating students about the Internet.

Another source of controversy is the potential for establishing inappropriate contacts through student use of e-mail, chat rooms, and other forms of interactive communication. While there is the potential for undesirable experiences resulting from Internet surfing, the Internet can also provide anyone access to current, specialized information that is unavailable in other types of resources. As with other issues, it is the sensationally bad experiences seen in the media that raise concerns and lead to public controversy that becomes a problem for school systems.

In an effort to ensure student safety, administrators should strive to develop policies that support appropriate instructional use but inhibit improper use. A decision to use a filter to limit access to inappropriate content can provide a false sense of security. There are three major shortcomings of filters. First, filters do not totally block inappropriate material. The terms the filter is designed to block can be circumvented by site developers by using seemingly safe terminology to literally entrap users by misdirecting valid search strategies. Second, filters block appropriate material because the filter cannot differentiate multiple meanings or contexts for the terms it blocks. While the term "adult" may mean X-rated to the filter, it also is used in connection with assigned topics such as "adult literacy," "adult learners" or any of a number of other topics with legitimate, useful information. Third is the matter of consensus regarding what is or is not appropriate for student access. Websites related to controversial topics have some very worthwhile parts but may also link to inappropriate material. Differences among community and family values create additional troublesome gray areas for schools to clarify. The librarian may or may not control the decision to filter. The district or other government unit may mandate filtering as a condition of funding. When filters are used, they do little to help students develop self-discipline; rather, they create a challenge for some students to defeat the filter.

In contrast, the widely used policies requiring parents and students to sign use agreements identifying acceptable behaviors and the consequences for misuse have proven to be an effective method of control. Such approaches help students realize that they need to develop the self-control needed to continue to have unrestricted access to information. The knowledge that consequences for misuse will be swift, consistent, and non-negotiable is an effective deterrent. Additionally, when students know supervisory staff can and do scan their monitors frequently, they are less likely to misuse their access privileges.

Controversy can be avoided when educators communicate the policies and practices related to student Internet access to parents and the communities. Trust is developed when parents are part of the process of developing the policies, when they understand the instructional benefits, and when they recognize that the school is alert to potential problems.

Can the Internet replace the school library?

Another type of controversy is related to academic use of the Internet as a research tool. Some people have a misconception that the Internet can replace all other library resources. The perception that any desired information is free, immediate, and accurate may or may not be true. Another misconception is that providing the hardware and connectivity is all that teachers and librarians need to integrate the Internet into the instructional program. In reality, it takes about three years to get a program running smoothly. A third misconception is that all teachers will recognize the value of integrating Internet use and choose to change their teaching style accordingly. These misconceptions have considerable impact on the ways that schools handle the implementation of the Internet in instructional settings.

Again, administrators must consider a series of decisions about how to make the most effective use of the instructional opportunities that Internet access provides. First and foremost is the need to accept that the Internet is not always the most appropriate resource to solve an information need. Often, a print resource, compact disc, video or online database contains the desired information. The strength of the Internet is access to very current, rapidly changing, or specialized information. However, one must weed out many non-productive hits before finding the usable resource. This becomes very time consuming and impractical. Students frequently lack sufficient background knowledge of the topic to make constructive choices when faced with hundreds and even thousands of potential sites.

In contrast to the unorganized Internet offerings, one can, for a fee, subscribe to electronic resources that are regularly updated to provide current information. Because these resources are designed to meet the needs of student researchers they have an organized structure and a level of reliable authenticity that the Internet does not. The cost can be prohibitive for some schools. This is why education departments in some states now license these types of resources and make them available to schools within the state.

For these reasons, many schools choose to establish a Web page with preselected sites identified for use with specific assignments. This approach ensures on-task and productive use of computer time. Posting information related to assignments, including rubrics for evaluation, sources to use, and timelines for completion on a school-generated Web page provides access to both students and interested parents. This type of communications link allows the community to understand how Internet use is integrated into classroom instruction.

Administrators must decide how to provide the training necessary to facilitate instructional use of the Internet and other electronic resources. Electronic resources demand search strategies that are very different from those used with traditional print resources. The need to create terms and identify interrelationships to initiate a key word search requires a different kind of thinking than the use of a traditional printed index. This in turn requires teachers to change what they present in order to model, provide guided practice with, and eventually require independent application of these skills in order to develop student mastery. Another result of the shift to reliance on electronic resources is the potential for plagiarism because of the ease of copy-and-paste procedures. Teachers recognize the need to emphasize bibliographic citation as a way to combat plagiarism. In all these areas, collaboration between the library media teacher and classroom teachers is the key to a consistent schoolwide approach.

Using the strategies in a real school

How do these strategies work in the real world?

The following case history shares my experience since 1995 in implementing Global Access (an education term for full infusion of technology) at one elementary building within a large school district. Many of the initial decisions were controlled by the central administration, including our being selected as one of five initial Global Access sites at the elementary level.

TECHNICAL DECISIONS

Given the need for systemwide equity and compatibility to facilitate support to participating schools, decisions as to total budget, choice of platform, type of network and connection, and a basic software collection were made at the system level. The district decided to provide elementary schools with networked Macintosh computers for all teaching stations within the building and a "research learning hub" of five, including a Power Mac with AV capability, for the media center. The county recommended placing multiple computers in each classroom rather than to create a computer lab.

All computers were configured to operate with the school's Winnebago circulation system and catalog. All had standard software including browsers, communications programs, word processing, desktop publishing, spreadsheet programs, and other applications. All machines had server access to *World Book Encyclopedia* on CD-ROM.

Decisions related to access and supervision including placement within the building, specific equipment to be purchased, and scheduling were made at the building level.

It was the staff consensus that access to a computer lab—allowing all students in a class to have simultaneous hands-on access—was a higher priority than having multiple computers in each classroom. We believed that lab access was necessary to facilitate teaching students to navigate the new software, complete writing activities in a reasonable amount of time, and provide supervised access to electronic resources. The priority for the staff was flexibility. The staff disagreed with the opinion of the central administration that use of a lab implies computer skills being taught in isolation and that all students would by necessity be doing the same activity regardless of need. We envisioned use of the lab facilitating integration of computer use into class work and providing opportunities for differentiation. Knowing the prevailing attitude toward computer labs, our local plan was written to include an ELF (Electronic Learning Facility) rather than a lab.

A variety of other hardware decisions included the purchase of peripherals including six laser printers distributed throughout the building, two scanners, two digital cameras, and six zip drives. Eighteen Powerbooks and two mini-hubs were purchased to support staff home use and the creation of portable mini-labs for classroom use. Other purchases included a class set of Alpha Smarts in a rolling cart and TV connectors for each classroom computer to facilitate class viewing of demonstration lessons.

The initial configuration for our building placed one Mac in each classroom and resource room. The Research Learning Hub in the media center consisted of seven computers, two of which are connected to scanners, zip drives, and a large-screen TV. The ELF houses two laser printers, and 32 Macs, one connected to an LCD projection device, and the Alpha Smart cart between classroom uses. The other laser printers are distributed throughout the building providing access from all classrooms. In addition to the instructional computers, the principal and both main office secretaries were provided with computer access. The servers are housed in the wire closet across the hall from the media center.

DECISIONS REGARDING ACCESS AND SUPERVISION

Staff in our school made the decision to require a staff logon and password to access the Internet to ensure supervised use by our elementary students. While this approach requires substantial prep time to ready the ELF for class use of the Internet, it was believed that since the county's policy was to not require acceptable use policies at the elementary level we needed to limit independent student access in order to build a relationship of trust with parents concerned about what they might have heard or read in the media.

We guide our student use of the Internet through bookmarks added by individual teachers, links provided through the county Web page, and suggested sites posted by the media specialist on the ELF bulletin board. The county Web page provides links organized by grade level areas and which support required units of study. The bulletin board provides annotated suggestions for sites to explore related to age appropriate topics of general interest. Teacher-initiated bookmarks support individual assignments relevant to their classes. Independent open-ended surfing is discouraged for a number of reasons. Besides the chance that young students will encounter inappropriate material, they often lack sufficient sophistication in search strategies to generate and spell keywords to initiate successful searches. Selecting the most useful sites from numerous hits and then reading the material is beyond many young students. It is important to select resources, including the Internet, for their ability to efficiently meet the instructional need. No format is inherently superior.

The importance of training

Our decisions related to training have made the biggest impact on teachers' willingness to integrate the use of technology into their instructional activities. As the first group of computers arrived in the building we set them up as temporary lab in the TV studio. Staff was given training related to basic Macintosh operations including use of the mouse, pull-down menus, highlighting, font selection, copy-and-paste procedures, etc. Staff participated in three days of voluntary training at the end of the school year with stipend pay provided. The content of this training focused on learning word processing skills, how to navigate *Kid Pix* and *First Class*, as well as exploring ideas for integrating these programs into traditional instructional activities. At the conclusion of the three days, teachers were given the opportunity to take one of the computers home for the summer. Trouble-shooting help was provided by the media specialist both by phone and through e-mail contact. Come fall the confidence level of much of the staff had increased dramatically.

Staff development funds were used to provide substitutes for periodic half-day release time by grade level for teachers to meet for additional focused technology training. Before and after school sessions were offered to introduce staff to use of a specific peripheral such as the scanner or digital camera or to introduce a new piece of software as our collection grew. One-on-one individualized training/planning for classroom application was offered during a teacher's planning time. Much of this training was presented by the media specialist with support from county level specialists.

Student skills were developed through a combination of strategies involving initial modeling, followed by guided practice and eventual independent application. Students learned new skills in either the ELF with individual students at their own computers, in the media center with small groups sharing a HUB computer, or in the classroom with demonstrations using the large screen TV. Collaboration between the media specialist and classroom teachers provided support for both the teacher and the students as their skills and confidence increased. Knowing that some students knew more than many teachers, trainers emphasized building a community of learners with the key assumption that the teaching and learning roles would at times be reversed.

During the initial year, we provided eight evening sessions for parents. Many of the evening sessions were designed for parent-child partners at specific grade levels to demonstrate instructional integration of various software programs. A parents-only session was held to share Internet activities, provide hands-on experience, and discuss related issues and concerns.

Training continues to be important. Individuals who have joined the staff since the initial training need to be given the opportunity to learn to use the technology available in our building that they may not have had access to previously. As new hardware and software are added to our collection and upgrades are installed training needs to be provided for all staff members. It is vital that teachers have confidence they can have help when they need it most. As with any major change, not all individuals progress at the same rate. Training and support must be provided when the individual is ready to take the next step forward. We have found that training without immediate application tends to be far less useful.

Minimizing frustration: Hardware and software support

Once teachers and students experience the impact technology can have on their daily teaching and learning, any interruption in access is a major frustration. As a Global Access school, we are provided with the regular services of a user support specialist. This individual is responsible for network management and maintenance, initial troubleshooting of computers and peripherals, and installation of new hardware, software, and upgrades of current software. On average, the user support specialist comes to our building three days a month. E-mail contact between visits can solve some types of problems. The media specialist can do much of the routine troubleshooting once the user support specialist has provided passwords to access the servers and hard drives. When a repair requiring replacement parts or substantial specialized knowledge is encountered, a call is placed to the help desk and county-contracted repairmen are scheduled to provide the required service.

As our hardware ages, we are experiencing more frequent need for repairs. Over the past five years we have added much in the way of adaptive technology to support our special education program. Specific hardware and software has been funded to allow our non-verbal students to begin to communicate. Utility software, content area CD-ROMs, and online resources have been expanded greatly to provide increased resources to support the instructional program. Due to ever-increasing reliance on electronic communication between the central office and individual school buildings, more powerful computers have been added to enhance this communication. Upgrades have also been made to our servers allowing us to save and access files from any computer within the building and discontinue use of discs by individuals as a primary means of storing and retrieving files.

The message to our students is to use and not abuse what we have as it will be a long time before the county funds any new major upgrades. All other buildings must first become Global Access schools before the initial schools will be revisited. With over 200 buildings in the district, it will be a number of years before we can expect another major investment in our site.

Tell parents and the community how you integrate technology into the curriculum

Once the hardware and software are available, decisions governing how access will be integrated into instruction need to become the major focus. Our staff has chosen to limit use of the Internet to what it does best, namely interacting with experts, observing phenomena, and locating current information not available in other formats. Information that is readily available in traditional print resources or other types of electronic tools is accessed in traditional ways. Internet projects are selected based on their ability to offer unique information of interest to a diverse group of students.

If the school's Internet use is to be managed well, staff must let parents and other community members know how they are using it to enhance education. Media frenzies are almost automatic when there is "inappropriate" usage by students, but how many times have you read coverage about projects like the two described below?

THE JOURNEY NORTH

The Journey North site is an example of one that we have been able to repeatedly integrate successfully into the curriculum of several grades. This site documents the seasonal changes associated with the arrival of Spring as the season moves from south to north across North America. Animal migration is documented with reported sightings of roughly a dozen species as is the disappearance of ice from bodies of water, the emergence of tree leaves, and the appearance of tulip blossoms. Students interact with experts by generating questions for the experts to answer and by attempting to answer challenge questions posed by the experts. Periodic updates of their observations are posted by the scientists along with biographical information and descriptions of their backgrounds, interests, and training. Interacting with this site provides authentic application of skills related to reading, math, science, and geography. Information literacy skills related to interpreting maps, charts, graphs, and text are strengthened. Participation in Journey North's mock monarch migration activity has been incorporated into our third grade study of Mexico and our second grade butterfly unit. Fourth graders studying our local Chesapeake Bay have focused on migrations of various marine animals including whales and manatees.

LITERATURE ACTIVITIES

Many author's pages are integrated into literature activities. *Stone Fox* by Gardiner is read by fourth graders during the running of the Iditarod dog sled race to integrate use of the Iditarod.com page to find daily updates of the race as it progresses. Sites providing views and descriptions of daily life in Japan are used with third graders during their unit on Japan. In most cases the class will be introduced to a new site by having it modeled. The layout of the pages and any special features the students will be expected to access will be demonstrated. Providing some sort of structure such as a pathfinder or set of questions is helpful for students when participating in guided practice activities. This type of support helps them stay focused on what it is you want students to experience. With practice, students can begin to independently apply the skills they have learned and begin to initiate successful searches on their own.

Based on printouts brought to school in connection with a variety of assignments, it is obvious that many of our students surf the Web extensively at home. It is the decision of our staff that while use of the Internet is highly motivational, in many cases it is not an efficient use of limited instructional time. Because of the age of our students and the level of their independent search skills, we choose to focus instruction on gathering relevant information from pre-selected quality sites. As students move into middle school and high school, the focus of instruction shifts to developing independent search strategies. Instruction at the secondary level includes teaching the use of appropriate keywords for successful searches, determining the accuracy and authenticity of Internet content, recognizing opinion and bias, and collecting and interpreting whether the information found matches the need.

CONCLUSION

The potential of the Internet to motivate students, to enrich teaching and learning, and to provide equity of access for all students is enormous. The potential for misuse is equally enormous. The instructional staff and administration, working with parents, must take the time to discuss the issues related to integrating Internet use and reach decisions that reflect what is valued. When the priority is put on teaching students to become effective users of electronic resources, students receive a lifetime of benefits. Students who learn to develop effective search strategies, to recognize the difference between quality information and unsubstantiated opinions or biased content, and to accept responsibility for ethical use of material will possess a major advantage in higher education, in the job market, and in the pursuit of personal interests. It is up to administrators and governing boards to make the appropriate choices related to providing access, training, and instruction to achieve the desired results for all students.

Chapter 12

Internet and Fort Vancouver Regional Library

Candace Morgan

Fort Vancouver Regional Library (FVRL) is an Intercounty Rural Library District established under the authority of Washington State Law (RCW 27.12.090). It provides public library service to twelve cities and the unincorporated areas of three counties. FVRL serves a population of over 350,000 residing in approximately 4,200 square miles in southwestern Washington. Twelve cities are included in the service district, ranging in population from 600 to 135,000. The governing and taxing authority for the library resides with the Library Board of Trustees, which is appointed by the county commissioners of the three counties served by the library (RCW 27.12.130, 150, 210).

BACKGROUND

Some background information is necessary to provide a context for the choices FVRL has made concerning public Internet access. In 1992–1993, Fort Vancouver Regional Library was involved in a long public process that began when the library purchased the book *Sex* by Madonna (Morgan, 1993). As an outcome of that process, the Library Board adopted a "Policy on Minor's Access to Library Materials." The library published the policy along with a documentation of the public process (Fort Vancouver Regional Library, 1993c). A training video was also produced, funded by the state library ("Libraries Under Fire," 1993). Shortly after the completion of the process, the library's "Policy for the Selection and Discarding of Materials" was reviewed and amended to include electronic resources (Fort Vancouver Regional Library, 1993b).

The board drew upon many resources to reach its decision not to restrict minors' access to the collection and to hold parents responsible for their own children's use of the library. Before reaching a decision, board members seriously considered a number of options, most of which were suggested by the community. The board's decision was supported by a majority of those who attended meetings or wrote, called, or telephoned to express an opinion. This method of decision-making was deliberately chosen in recognition of the library's role at the juxtaposition between two important constitutional values—individual liberties and majority rule.

The board announced at the beginning of the process that it would take no action that violates the federal or state constitutional guarantees of free speech. However, the board members asked the community to participate in a process to study ways that the library might provide assistance for parents who wish to guide the reading of their own minor children. The board held a forum on children's access issues that included a staff presentation on the historical, legal, and constitutional framework. Policy Committee members spent a total of over 200 hours reviewing information provided by staff and the public. They put forth possible policies and discussed their relationship to existing policies as well as the possible consequences of the adoption of proposed changes to the policy. They wrote a report to the full board that was widely circulated, and they held two public meetings to discuss it. In addition, time was set aside at each monthly board meeting for public comments. Staff and board members spoke at a number of organization and club meetings, providing background on the issue. The library provided information to local newspapers and persuaded a local cable company to film the public meetings. Copies of the city cable videos were added to the library's collection.

The entire staff was included in the process. Work-group staff meetings were planned to include interactive discussions concerning the issue and staff experiences on the job. We wanted staff to feel comfortable discussing the issue, including the legal and constitutional background. The staff members represent a wide range of ages and backgrounds and, of course, live throughout our three-county, 4,200–square-mile service area. Coming from quite differing perspectives, the staff helped develop a flexible repertoire of ways to discuss the issues without quoting policy or law directly.

The development of the "Minors' Access Policy" was

contentious and laborious, but it was a local process and created a model for how the library might deal with future community-wide controversy concerning collection or services. This model includes (not necessarily in this order):

- Identifying the issue(s)
- Analyzing constitutional and legal requirements
- Examining current policy
- Developing options
- Involving community and staff
- Keeping the community informed

INTERNET

By 1995, library management and the board agreed that public access to the Internet in the library would enhance the library's historical mission of providing diverse information from all points of view to enable library users to make individual choices.

Starting with current policy

Internet access was launched in the fall of 1995. A specific Internet policy was not adopted. It was determined that the access section of the selection policy and the library's rules of conduct provided adequate policy coverage to begin Internet access. The library wanted direct experience with the service and time to use that information to determine what, if any, additional policies were needed.

To assist individuals who want to have guidance in using the Internet, library reference staff developed a home page with links to reference and information sites. The library's youth services specialists developed links to sites intended for young people. These links were chosen within the guidelines of the library's selection policy.

Public response to the availability of Internet access terminals was so positive that staff almost immediately established time limits on individual use of the Internet to enable as many people as possible to use the service. After several instances of people inadvertently observing someone else viewing something they found objectionable, we installed privacy screens on all the terminals (we are now using recessed monitors). In the latter half of 1997, after we had received some public requests to have software filters available, library staff identified a number of filtered search engines and directories on the Internet and linked them to the library's home page so individuals would have that choice.

In early 1998, a resident of a nearby community (who is not a resident of the library's taxing district) began a campaign to force FVRL to install software filters on all its Internet terminals to keep people from accessing what she termed "pornography." Partially because of the attention generated by this challenge in the media, but more because they thought that it was time, the Library Board began a process involving staff and the public to study the library's Internet access policies and procedures.

Identifying the issues

At the March 1998 board meeting, staff presented a background report on the Internet and software filtering. Fol-

lowing the model of policy review established in 1992, the
Board Policy Committee began an intensive study of the
Internet and filtering issues. The most significant problem
to be addressed was whether FVRL should install software
filters on the Internet terminals, either for all users or for
children.

Exploring options

By this time, considerable evidence had accumulated that
filters do not work very well. All available filters block
some sites that most people would not find objectionable
and fail to filter sites that many people would find ques-
tionable. No filter exists that can exclude only constitutionally unprotected speech. The board, however, wanted
to get first-hand information. A lab was set up for use by
the board and staff with a number of filters to try out. Information was gathered about what other libraries were
doing and about the constitutional issues involved. The
board solicited public comment in a number of forums.

As library staff and board members examined and discussed issues related to Internet access and filtering in
preparation for policy development, it became apparent
that the American constitutional legacy of unfettered personal choice was the major defining issue. A free people
should be able to choose how they search the Internet, sug-
gesting that filtering should not be mandated. However,
filters should be available as a choice. As long as the limitations of filters are explained, people should have the right
to have this tool made available with tax money. Spending tax money only on unfiltered Internet access could also
be considered a violation of equal protection. Unfortu-

nately, the technology did not exist at the time of the board's decision to make it possible for the Internet searcher on a library terminal to make the choice between filtered and unfiltered searching in a cost effective manner.

Involving community and staff

The Policy Committee used all the information that had been gathered and drafted a "Policy on Access to Electronic Information" (Fort Vancouver Regional Library, 1998) that was then subject to a public hearing and a public open comment period. Staff members discussed their experiences working with the public using the Internet and generally agreed that the draft policy could be successfully implemented. After three months of public input and study, the policy was adopted in August 1998.

The "Policy on Access to Electronic Resources" states that the library will not impose blocking or filtering software to limit access to Internet sites. However, on all Internet terminals the Library will provide users with the option of using search engines or mechanisms that provide access only to pre-selected sites. This option is intended to assist all patrons in meeting their special interests or their own family values (Ibid). The policy also states:

> The use of all library resources, including electronic resources, is voluntary. The Library does not select the material on the Internet and has no way to assure that only constitutionally protected material is available on the Internet. Access to, use of, or dissemination of constitutionally unprotected speech in the Library, in vio-

lation of this policy, is the responsibility of the user, or in the case of minors it is a joint responsibility of the user and the parent or guardian.

Integrating new and old policies

Holding library users responsible for following the law in the ways that they use materials available in or through the library is similar to the way the library works within the copyright law. The library provides access to materials that are, or may be, copyrighted and warns library users that the receiver of the materials has the legal obligation to follow copyright law. Parental responsibility for their children's use of the Internet parallels library policy on parental responsibility for their own children's access to other library materials and services.

Exploring technological options for implementing policy

During the public-comment stage, there was strong support for not using the government's power to mandate filtered access to the Internet in the library. Concerns were raised, however, about how parents can reasonably take responsibility for their own children's access to the Internet. Therefore, the policy directed library staff to explore the availability of effective and economically feasible technology to enable parents to limit their own minor children's use of electronic resources in the library. Staff were also directed to take steps to protect the privacy of Internet users.

The exploration of ways to assist parents in response to the board mandate required that library staff frame the issues related to children using the Internet. Minors do have First Amendment rights but the Supreme Court has ruled that state legislation may specify that some materials that are protected for adults may be considered "obscene" for minors (Jenner & Block, 1998). However, since Washington State's "harmful to minors" law was found to be unconstitutional in 1994 (*Soundgarden v Eikenberry* 123 Wash 2d 750), any action taken by staff directly to limit children's access to the Internet would raise issues of unconstitutional government censorship. Thus, staff determined that we needed to find a technological way to enable parents to control the way their children search the Internet without using staff to act as the parent.

Throughout the library's "experimental" time with Internet access prior to formulating the policy, the most frequent difficulties encountered by staff were related to the time limits and Internet users who did not close out all sites before leaving the terminal. As a result of these problems staff selected a vendor of Internet management software, Pharos *(www.pharos.com)*, to provide the library with software that would address these issues specifically. The library decided that it would be most cost effective to explore whether the Pharos software could be developed further to address the issues related to parental guidance.

Making choices consistent with other policies

To determine how to approach providing technological methods for parents to make Internet searching choices for their children, staff members examined related policies and practices. It was decided that linking the choice of filtered or unfiltered Internet access to the library card number was the best choice because that method would be consistent with current practice concerning access to patron data in the circulation system.

When individuals register for a library card, staff tell them that anyone who has the card and its PIN can use that information to check the cardholder record on the OPAC, including items checked out and on hold. Children do not need a parental signature to get a card, but if they do not have identification, someone else with a library card must identify them. In reality most young children register with a parent or other adult to whom the parent has entrusted them. When families register together we suggest they determine how they will handle access to each cardholder record since staff will not reveal the information to anyone other than the person in possession of the card. This has worked well. We believe that it reasonably balances the conflicting values of children's rights and parental responsibility.

Following this model, staff asked Pharos to expand the software so that each person who registers as an Internet user chooses the environment within which she or he wishes to search (unfiltered or filtered). That choice becomes the default each time the user signs up to use the Internet. The choice can be password protected so a parent can use his or her child's library card to select the search environment for the child and then password it. This choice is linked to the child's library card number, so the parent needs to make that choice only once.

Informing the community

FVRL has taken a number of steps to inform the public

of the Internet searching choices available on library terminals and the steps that parents can take to control their children's access to the Internet. The Pharos software was activated one branch at a time and each time press releases were sent to all local media. Staff responded to requests to speak to organizations. Informational flyers were mailed to all households in the FVRL service area. English and Spanish versions of the flyer are available at all branches.

During the public discussion of the policy we became aware that many parents do not know enough about how the Internet works to provide guidance for their children. A committee composed of library staff and several members of the public is designing a training program for parents that will provide them with information about the Internet. This process will better prepare parents to guide their children's use of the Internet and to exercise the choices available to them in the library. Library staff will train community volunteers to provide much of this training, an approach that the library anticipates will help keep it connected to the community on this issue.

Has the process of developing an Internet policy been successful in balancing conflicting values? It is too early for a definitive judgment, however the indications are positive. In March 2000, eight months after FVRL began to use the Pharos software, 20 percent of registered Internet users have chosen filtered access. Those who demanded that the library filter all Internet terminals, or at least require that all minors use filters, are not satisfied. Most Internet users registered as they were requested to do so with little comment. We have received many positive comments from members of the public, as well as several positive editorial opinions in local newspapers.

CONCLUSION

The freedom of each individual to choose which ideas and information to access in the library and on the Internet, participatory government, and majority rule are all fundamental constitutional values of the United States. As a community-based governmental institution with a core mission of protecting the First Amendment rights of all citizens, the American public library sometimes finds itself at the point of conflict between individual rights and actual or perceived community values. This has certainly been the case with the Internet.

None of the recently enacted federal or state laws intended to restrict access to Internet content have successfully passed constitutional challenge (Freedom to Read Foundation, 2000). This situation is frustrating for parents who wish to guide their child's use of the Internet. This study of Fort Vancouver Regional Library's development of policies and procedures for public Internet access is an example of how public libraries have an opportunity to use community based decision-making to develop policies that help to reconcile constitutional imperatives and local community concerns.

RESOURCES

Fort Vancouver Regional Library. 1993a. *Libraries Under Fire: A Case Study.* Vancouver, WA: MVP Video Productions, Inc.

Fort Vancouver Regional Library. 1993b. *Policy for the Selection and Discarding of Materials*, August 16.

Vancouver, WA: Fort Vancouver Regional Library.

Fort Vancouver Regional Library. 1993c. *Policy on Minor's Access to Library Materials*, January 29. Vancouver, WA: Fort Vancouver Regional Library.

Fort Vancouver Regional Library. 1998. *Policy on Access to Electronic Information*, August 10. Vancouver, WA: Fort Vancouver Regional Library.

Freedom to Read Foundation. 2000. *FTRF reports to ALA Council.* [Online]. Available: *www.ftrfreports.html.*

Jenner & Block. 1998. *Application of "Community Standards" Component of Legal Obscenity Test to Librarians' Internet Communications; Memorandum to the American Library Association.* [Online]. Available at: *www.ala.org/alaorg/oif/app_jb.html.*

Morgan, Candace. 1993. "Who's on First?" *Alki: The Washington Library Association Journal*: 9–20.

Appendix

Checklist & Ideas For Library Staff Working With Community Leaders

Reprinted courtesy of the American Library Association

A. Local Library Board of Trustees

❑ Develop an educational session on intellectual freedom to orient new Board members as they are elected. Include:
  ❑ Overview of the role of libraries in democracy
    American Library Basics
    http://www.ala.org/alaorg/oif/americanlibrarybasics.html
  ❑ Discuss basic First Amendment principles
    Intellectual Freedom Q & A
    http://www.ala.org/alaorg/oif/
    intellectualfreedomandcensorship.html
  ❑ Highlight laws and legislation relevant to libraries and intellectual freedom
    Notable First Amendment Cases
    http://www.ala.org/alaorg/oif/lstcases.html
  ❑ Legal Memoranda to the Freedom to Read Foundation
    http://www.ftrf.org/memos-jb.html
  ❑ Explain the role of the Board, to:
    ❑ Work with the Library Director to ensure that the neces-

sary policies are in place and that they are reviewed regularly and thoroughly
- ❏ Review and affirm the library selection policy annually and make sure it is followed carefully
- ❏ Be an effective advocate for the library. Use your contacts in the community to educate and mobilize others in support of the library
- ❏ Bring what you hear back to the Library Director
- ❏ Distribute copies of key documents:
  - ❏ *Library Bill of Rights*
    http://www.ala.org/work/freedom/lbr.html
  - ❏ Libraries: An American Value
    http://www.ala.org/alaorg/oif/lib-val.html
  - ❏ ALA Libraries & the Internet Toolkit
    http://www.ala.org/internettoolkit/index.html
  - ❏ *Intellectual Freedom Manual*
    Available from ALA editions, http://alastore.ala.org/
  - ❏ *Libraries, the First Amendment, and Cyberspace: What You Need to Know* by Robert Peck
    Available from ALA editions, http://alastore.ala.org/
- ❏ Present an orientation to the Internet. Include:
- ❏ Filters and Filtering
  http://www.ala.org/alaorg/oif/filtersandfiltering.html
  - ❏ What is the Internet?
  - ❏ How is it useful?
  - ❏ Explain your Internet use policy
  - ❏ Address Internet filters, what they are and how they work
- ❏ Update the Board regularly with local and national news clippings, include Internet success stories, pending legislation, court cases, etc.
- ❏ Distribute information on educational programs
- ❏ Encourage personal/institutional membership in ALA and the Freedom to Read Foundation
- ❏ Provide subscription to *The Newsletter on Intellectual Freedom* for the Board
  http://www.ala.org/alaorg/oif/nif-inf.html
- ❏ Supply suggested reading lists on intellectual freedom issues from professional journals and books (e.g., *Libraries, Access,*

and Intellectual Freedom by Barbara M. Jones; *Libraries, The First Amendment and Cyberspace*, by Robert S. Peck; *Protecting the Right to Read* by Ann K. Symons and Charles Harmon; bibliographies found in the *Newsletter on Intellectual Freedom*)

B. Friends of the Library

❏ Prepare an orientation on intellectual freedom issues in libraries:
  ❏ Overview of the role of libraries in democracy
    American Library Basics
    http://www.ala.org/alaorg/oif/americanlibrarybasics.html
  ❏ Highlight basic First Amendment principles
    Intellectual Freedom Q & A
    http://www.ala.org/alaorg/oif/
    intellectualfreedomandcensorship.html
  ❏ Explain the role of Friends vs. the role of the Board
❏ Distribute copies of key intellectual freedom documents:
  ❏ *The Library Bill of Rights*
    http://www.ala.org/work/freedom/lbr.html
  ❏ Intellectual Freedom and Censorship Q & A
    http://www.ala.org/alaorg/oif/
    intellectualfreedomandcensorship.html
  ❏ Provide bibliographies of suggested reading on intellectual freedom
    Books on the Internet and Intellectual Freedom
    http://www.ala.org/alaorg/oif/internetbooks.html
    Newsletter on Intellectual Freedom
    http://www.ala.org/alaorg/oif/nif - inf.html
  ❏ Prepare orientation to the Internet for Friends officers
    Filters and Filtering
    http://www.ala.org/alaorg/oif/filtersandfiltering.html
  ❏ What is the Internet?
  ❏ How is it useful?
  ❏ Explain your Internet use policy
  ❏ Address Internet filters, what they are and how they work
❏ Demonstrate the value of the Internet at Friends events
❏ Provide updates on local news of interest, include Internet successes and relevant legislation

C. Elected/Appointed Officials and their Staffs/Administration of Academic Institutions and their Staffs

❏ Provide Internet demonstrations, tailor examples to information that is relevant to their jobs and responsibilities
❏ Build relationships by offering to train staff on topics of expertise (e.g., how to conduct a reference interview—and discover what your clients really want!)
❏ Orient to legal issues pertaining to intellectual freedom, include national and local laws, and relevant legislation
   http://www.ala.org/alaorg/oif/first.html
❏ Provide legal updates on intellectual freedom cases in other jurisdictions
   http://www.freedomforum.org/
❏ Encourage institutional memberships in ALA, FTRF, state and regional library associations
❏ Offer library support for their information needs
❏ Prepare and distribute packets of library statistics that demonstrate the value of the library to the community (e.g., patrons per day, Internet sessions per day, reference counts, etc.)

D. Local Media

❏ Offer library support for information needs
❏ Invite to Friends orientation sessions/Internet demonstrations
❏ Provide updates on intellectual freedom legal issues
❏ Provide updates on local events, role of library in community
❏ Submit op-ed pieces
   http://w3.trib.com/FACT/1st.oped.html
❏ Invite to open houses/library tours

E. Local Citizen Groups and Potential Allies (e.g., ministerial associations, civic groups, ACLU, local educators, university professors, service clubs)

❏ Offer library support for information needs
❏ Invite to Friends orientation sessions/Internet demonstrations
❏ Offer to be or provide a speaker for club meetings
❏ Update on local intellectual freedom issues, including Internet successes and pending legislation
❏ Recruit potential members of the Board of Trustees of Friends Board from these groups

Permission is granted to libraries to reproduce this checklist.

Reprinted courtesy of the American Library Association © 2000

About the Authors

Carolyn Caywood has been a librarian for 28 years, the last 20 as a manager for the Virginia Beach Public Library in Virginia. She is a graduate of Wayne State University, currently a member of the Freedom to Read Foundation Board, and, in 1993, a founder of a local public user group, the Hampton Roads Internet Association. From 1990 through 1998 she wrote a column on teen library services for *School Library Journal*.

Gordon M. Conable is former president of the Freedom to Read Foundation and a past chair of the ALA Intellectual Freedom Committee. While Conable was Director of the Monroe County (Michigan) Library System, that library system provided patrons with free Internet accounts and quickly became the largest Internet Service Provider in the county.

Susan Fuller has directed the Santa Clara County Library in California since 1985. She was the *Library Journal* Librarian of the Year for 1999 and California Library Association Librarian of the Year for 1997.

Melissa Henderson has 10 years' experience in electronic publishing, including as marketing manager for Chadwyck-Healey Inc. and as library marketing manager for *Congressional Quarterly*. She was the online content director for the National PTA for four years where she led the development of award-winning Websites focusing on child advocacy issues. Currently, Henderson works for the North Suburban Library System as the coordinator of the NorthStarNet community information network, which includes more than 60 public libraries in the North Suburban Library System and provides Web-hosting services for more than 1,000 organizations in 120 communities.

M. Ellen Jay has been a school media specialist for Montgomery County Public Schools for 30 years. For the last five years her school has been fully networked with Internet access from all teaching stations. She has been responsible for training staff and students, designing instructional interactions which integrate use of technology and collection development to support use of computers. Dr. Jay served as 1999–2000 President of the American Association of School Librarians and is the author of numerous books and articles.

Nancy Kranich, President of the American Library Association for the 2000–2001 year, is the Associate Dean of Libraries at New York University. Kranich has made more than 200 presentations and written more than 60 articles on topics related to digital libraries, the information superhighway, freedom of information, access, equity, scholarly communication, government information and telecommunications policy, fees for library service, evaluation of library services, and legislative action for librarians.

Judith Krug is the founding Director of the American Library Association's Office for Intellectual Freedom and the founding Executive Director of the Freedom to Read Foundation. A prolific author and speaker, she is widely regarded as the nation's foremost authority on First Amendment issues in libraries.

Sarah Ann Long, the 1999–2000 President of the American Library Association, is the Director of the North Suburban Library System, an organization of 660 academic, public, school, and special libraries in the north/northwest suburbs of Chicago. During her 25 years of library service, Long has been the recipient of many awards including the Illinois Library Association Librarian of the Year for 1999. She is the author of numerous articles on library management, diversity, and other topics.

Candace Morgan has been Associate Director for Community Library Services at the Fort Vancouver Regional Library District in Vancouver, Washington since 1983. She has a Master's in Library Service (Columbia University) and a Master's in Public Administration (Lewis & Clark College) and is President of the Freedom to Read Foundation Board of Trustees (1999–2001).

Carolyn Noah is the Youth Services Consultant and Assistant Administrator at the Central Massachusetts Regional Library System in Shrewsbury. She is the chair of the Association for Library Services to Children's (ALSC) Intellectual Freedom Committee, a member of the ALSC Board of Directors, and author of "A Perfect Match: Children and the Internet," available on ALA's Website. Carolyn frequently conducts training for library staff on kids' access to information.

Patricia Glass Schuman is President and co-founder of Neal-Schuman Publishers, Inc. She has served as both Treasurer and President (1990–1991) of the American Library Association. Ms. Schuman is one of the nation's leading experts on library advocacy and frequently presents workshops and lectures on library advocacy, marketing, and public relations.

Mark Smith, author of the *Internet Policy Handbook for Libraries* (Neal-Schuman, 1999) is a regional manager for Library Systems and Services (LSSI) in the Riverside County (California) Library System. Previously, Smith served as the Director of Communications for the Texas Library Association and as a grants administrator for the Texas State Library and Archives Commission, where he participated in early efforts to provide Internet services to Texas public libraries.

Ann K. Symons, 1998–1999 President of the American Library Association, is a familiar library voice on filtering and Internet management issues. She has chaired ALA's Intellectual Freedom Committee, is currently a member of the Freedom to Read Foundation Board, and is the 2000 winner of the Robert B. Downs Intellectual Freedom

Award. Symons is the author of numerous articles as well as co-author of *Protecting the Right to Read: A How-To-Do-It Manual for School and Public Librarians* (Neal-Schuman, 1995) and co-editor of *Speaking Out: Voices in Celebration of Intellectual Freedom* (ALA Editions, 1999).

Index